JACOB

VEGAN FOOD PIMP COOKBOOK

A collection of vegan recipes and stories
from my time at Jacobs Ridge

COOKING IS LOVE MADE VISIBLE.

Printed in the United Kingdom

First Printing, 2016

ISBN 978-1-68419-509-1

Contact and enquiries at
www.veganfoodpimp.com

Facebook: veganfoodpimp
YouTube: veganfoodpimp

FOR MEGAN AND FREDDIE

So you never have a reason not to cook...
because you give me the energy to do what I do...
and most of all because
I love you both with everything I am.

X X X

ACKNOWLEDGEMENTS

BOOK DESIGN

Lisa Bennett

I have no words for just how much Lisa has helped get this book out there. She has worked around the clock to help produce my first book and I will be eternally grateful to my wonderful, new found sister. Big hugs and love forever, my friend.

BOOK EDITED BY

Megan Nicholson

PHOTOGRAPHS

Lynn Nicholson
Julian Nicholson
Megan Nicholson
Freddie Nicholson
Abbie Clover
Francis Sales
Debbie Zietman

MY INSPIRATION

My family
My animals
Nature

SPICES

www.steenbergs.co.uk

I cannot begin to explain just incredibly helpful Sophie Steenberg has been. Over the years, she has sent me all kinds of spices for me to experiment with and no matter what spice I requested, she would supply it. So a huge, huge thank you for all your support and long may our connection continue.

xxx

WHEN I COOK

I cook with purpose. I only cook vegan food.

My passion comes from a love of food and a love of animals.

I do not prepare vegan options. For me, there is only one option.

My aim is to make vegan mainstream, an everyday option,
not just a lifestyle choice.

This book brings you some of my recipes along some of my animal
friends who are a constant source of inspiration.

Be inspired, make change, go vegan.

VFP
xxx

JACOBS RIDGE

Creating Jacobs Ridge was an organic process.

It was never intended that we would own and run an animal sanctuary, but circumstances moved in a way that directed us, and ultimately we opened up the doors of our home to others.

2015 was the first year we had volunteers come and join us for a mix of volunteering and a holiday. Places sold out quickly. People loved being with the animals, the nature, the food and of course, with other like minded people. Jacobs Ridge became a place where people could just "be," without judgement.

We were proud to be a vegan destination, despite people telling us it would never work. We feel that anyone running a sanctuary should be vegan – how can you help some animals and eat others? We were right in sticking to our principles as a family. Through the support of our volunteers during 2015 and 2016, we have been able to rescue even more animals and the Ridge continues to grow.

Part of the profits from VFP will go directly to helping the animals at the Ridge and with everyone working together, we can all continue to make change to so many lives. You can read some of the Ridge animals' stories in this book.

Julian continues to look for new ways to improve and expand the Ridge and has made so many changes already. However, growth can only be achieved with your support, so do look at the website and book to visit. Through buying this book you are already helping, so from all of us, thank you and keep spreading the word.

www.jacobsridge.com

XX

This book is dedicated to **Nero**, who will always be in my heart.

I am vegan because I love animals. Not just some animals, all animals. When you look into the eyes of a pig, cow, chicken, horse, dog, turkey, cat – in fact, any animal – you feel connection.

When I prepared food at Jacobs Ridge for all our guests, no words needed to be spoken. People had spent the day with the animals and then they sat down around the table to talk about their experiences, which always included a funny story or two about the animals.

Those who were not vegan soon understood the connection between our extended family and the food they put onto their plates back home. Through eating wonderful vegan food and spending time with all our animals they made their own connection. It is through connection and education that change takes place.

I hope you enjoy meeting some of our animal family through the pages of this book and appreciate them for who they are. Equals.

XX

INTRODUCTION

Cooking has always been a passion.

It is my personal outlet, my personal method of relaxation, my opportunity to escape.

I learnt to cook from my Nan and most importantly my Mum. Her recipe books still sit on my shelf with her notes and scribblings and are some of my most treasured possessions. No matter how long she had been working, or what type of day she had, she would always produce a fresh, home cooked meal. She taught me how to love food, to enjoy food, to take something simple and create something wonderful. Mealtimes were special; family time, sitting around a table talking about the day, issues, problems, anything but always whilst sharing great food... Connection is so important.

At school I studied food and nutrition and later in life, I studied holistic nutrition, enabling me to create not only delicious dishes but healthy ones too!

My recipe book collection is huge – anything can be made into a vegan alternative. In the future I hope that people will consider vegan food an option just as they do Italian, Greek or Asian. Even if people only eat vegan once or twice a week it all makes a difference, but to make that happen people need to be attracted to the food, which – for me – is the challenge I love.

People that love food inspire me too, as does the challenge of creating something people think is impossible. I truly love working with food and feeding people, hence the nickname "Food Pimp".

Getting Started

Before you enter your kitchen, take a deep breath, take several, be calm, be organised and tap into your passion for food. All food tastes so much better when made with passion and love.

See food as an extension of who you are.

I have eaten in a few vegan restaurants and to be honest, most have been pretty disappointing, which is a huge shame as anyone who ventured in as a "meat eater" would probably have found the food bland and uninteresting when in fact, vegan food can literally sing off the plate. You just need to inject passion into the food you are preparing.

I have a few simple rules when it comes to cooking :

- Use fresh ingredients.

- Cook food you like. In my opinion, it is impossible to create a wonderful dish if you honestly hate what you are making; it will show up in the final result.

- Make life simple for yourself.

- Think ahead, make bigger portions – this way you have something for the next day which can be tweaked to create a whole new dish or you can freeze half for another day.

- Make use of spices and seasoning, be generous with them.

- Never throw anything away, any leftovers can be used to create another dish!

Equipment

I believe you only need a food processor and a good knife! When buying your food processor, do not go for the most expensive. Go for the one with the biggest bowl. Since mine gets a serious hammering I go for the best of the cheapest options. You can whip up so much in a food processor in no time at all and it makes all the difference. That, and a good knife, and you have everything you need.

Spices

Yes, these can be expensive, but you do not have to buy everything at once, just drop one or two into your weekly shop and very soon you have quite a collection. For me the main dry spices are oregano, turmeric, chili flakes, garlic, onion and paprika. This is a good start. Always buy basil and coriander fresh, nothing comes anywhere near the taste of these two favourites, fresh all the way!

Nuts, Dried Fruits, Seeds, Grains & Pulses

My shelves are stocked with bottles of ready cooked pulses, honestly, no one has the time, or the memory in my case, to remember to soak pulses the day before and nor do I have the time to cook them for days, either. Having pulses at hand means you can always knock something up quickly whilst getting that all important protein at the same time. Just pick up a couple of jars each time you shop and experiment with all types.

Nuts are a staple so always chuck a bag or two of different nuts into your trolley. I like to keep handy peanuts, almonds, whole, ground and flaked, cashews, walnuts and hazelnuts. You will be amazed at just how different food can taste with the added addition of a handful of nuts.

The same applies to dried fruits. You can lift so many dishes with the added addition of dried cranberries, apricots, prunes and dates. Even if you first think that you do not like some of these I have heard so many people telling me that they have always hated dates but loved them in a tagine, so try different things.

Seeds are so important and I tuck them into all sorts of things. Pumpkin, sesame and sunflower seeds should be kept in jars. Whenever you see these on promotion buy them, you will use them in a million things as they add texture, taste and nutrition to a million things!

Important Store Cupboard Ingredients

Nutritional Yeast

Now this is something that every vegan should have on their shelf. Never just go for a simple spoonful of it in cooking; be bold, tip it in! It adds so much flavour, it can be used for thickening and of course, it makes a wonderful parmesan cheese alternative that you will find within this book!

Marmite

I would just like to stress that I personally hate Marmite, so do not be put off by the idea of Marmite in your cooking. By adding it to dishes, you add colour and a depth of flavour that is unique. This you do use with caution – too much is really just too much!

Peanut Butter

Again, not something I like in a sandwich or on toast but as an addition to many dishes it makes a huge difference so always have a jar handy or even better, make your own, you will find a recipe in here for this too!

Coconut Milk

When you see this on offer, buy as much as you can! You can use it for so many things, not just curry either. How long has it been since you had a banoffee pie?

Liquid Smoke

This you can buy easily and it adds that barbecue taste to many things, lifting burgers to a new level! Go easy with this, too much and you will taste nothing but smoke!

Rice & Couscous

Always have rice and couscous available. You can always whip something up, particularly if you have leftovers. Buy a good selection of rice: wild rice, basmati or jasmine, for example. Always keep a big bag of couscous ready. Five minutes and you have a good base for a dish and you can always use leftovers for lunch the next day.

Noodles

I always keep these on my shelves. You can buy some brilliant ones that can make a meal look incredible; including black noodles, which add a whole new dimension. Very quick and easy to cook and perfect for a quick stir fry. Any leftover noodles can be used in a wrap or deep fried and sprinkled with lemon salt for a quick snack!

You will find my main supplier at the back of this book. Since I live in Spain, all of the stockists deliver here, so no excuses for not being able to get ingredients. If you live in the UK or the States you are probably spoilt for choice as to where you can buy your ingredients. Spain is improving; main supermarkets now stock plant based milks and even tofu! The smaller health food shops stock loads of things, including coconut oil. I buy lots of ingredients from small Moroccan shops who sell things like cashew nuts in larger quantities with a much better price tag and loads of different spices too. So, do your research and build your own directory of places to shop.

Recipes!

My recipes are in no order at all. When I cook, as you will know if you have been with me – I go from how I feel. I never plan ahead, which is why all these recipes can be prepared on the day. No soaking, no overnight fiascos, just grabbing everything and pulling it together.

It also depends on what is in season, what is on special and where my creative juices take me. Be the same – be spontaneous. I often hear people telling me that they cannot cook, but this is simply not true. Anyone can cook, it is about practice and gaining confidence. Never walk into a kitchen thinking you cannot cook as the results will just confirm it. Walk into a kitchen confident, strong and excited; the difference, I promise, will show in your food.

VEGAN FOOD PIMP xx

LET'S COOK

THESE ARE JUST DELICIOUS AND YOU CAN AMEND THE FLAVOURS TO SUIT YOUR OWN PERSONAL TASTE.

ARANCINI - RICE BALLS

YOU WILL NEED

Cooked rice (any rice works)

Bread crumbs

Liquid from a can of chickpeas and the rest, see right

Vegan cheese (optional)

The important thing in making Arancini is that the rice needs to be cooked in advance and it needs to be cold so you can manipulate it.

I invested in a rice cooker, best thing I ever did, put it all in there, which takes minutes, turn it on and leave it and then the next day you have your rice ready to go.

TO MAKE

1. In a big bowl add your rice. Now, again, not really big on measurements here. Use your common sense – the more rice you have, the more balls you have. You want to make them about the size of a tennis ball for a main dish, or if you want them to be a starter or party food, just make them smaller, like a golf ball.

2. So, rice in the bowl and now you add all your seasoning. Lots of salt and black pepper, dried garlic and onion powder, paprika, oregano, sesame seeds. In fact, just go with it; add what you have and create your own taste.

3. Once you have this mixture together, you need to scoop up a handful and mould into a ball. You can, at this point, add a piece of vegan cheese to the middle which will then melt as you cook them; it adds a new, delicious dimension.

4. Once you have created your ball, you need to roll it in the chickpea juice (works the same as egg white) and then roll into bread crumbs and set aside ready to cook. Keep going until you have made them all. Remember; these are great cold also, so do not worry about making so many.

5. You really do need to do these in a deep fat fryer for them to work, but you can heat up oil in a pan – just be super careful. However, to get the full effect, use a deep fat fryer every time. Granted, not overly healthy but you are not eating them everyday.

6. To cook them, carefully place them in your deep fat fryer, one or two at a time, until golden and then put into a warm oven.

Serve with a spicy tomato sauce or anything that you love.

 **TIP**

I know I go on about seasoning, but you really do need to get a little heavy handed with this one. Think about it, we are dealing with boiled rice, it needs oodles to bring it to life. So forget measuring – just go with your gut and I always add a vegetable stock cube to the water to give it extra taste, too.

NERO

IN MY WORLD.....

...its normal to talk to animals

Nero and Freddie

"NERO NEEDS A HOME"

I still smile to myself when I think of how Nero came into our lives. I remember so clearly Megan saying to me "Mum, we should have a donkey". I replied that if we were meant to have a donkey, it would find its way to us. The universe went to work.

Meg, Fred and I went to the local shop to pick up a few bits and bobs. I picked up an English newspaper and took it to the counter. The chap behind the counter told me that it was last week's paper and that the new ones would be in tomorrow, to which I replied, "Don't worry, it's just something to flick through."

We got home, I put the newspaper down and went about my day. That evening I picked up the paper with a cup of coffee and there, on the front page, was a picture of a donkey with the heading "Nero Needs A Home". I have to admit, at that point I knew he was special and he was meant to be with us.

Julian was away filming and as usual, his last words to us were, "No more animals!" but this was different. Nero was meant to be with us and I was sure he would understand, but I did not say anything because to be honest, I thought maybe, since this was last week's paper he already had a home.

I showed Megan who said, "Mum, you have to call – we asked for a donkey and here he is!"

I called the number and it turned out he was staying at Easy Horse Care Rescue, based in Spain also. They had rescued him after he had been left on a roundabout for three days. It turns out whilst he was a lovely donkey, he did not get on well with other donkeys (that never changed throughout the

whole time he was with us) and therefore they needed to find him a home. They said he was about 12 years old and so far they had received 1500 requests to re-home him!

We carried on talking and then I mentioned Hamlet. Sue, the lady who co owns the rescue centre, knew Hamlet's previous owner and said if I was good enough to have Hamlet then she was happy to send him to us. I was over the moon. The only other hurdle was Julian, but he understood and it was settled.

At that time we had one horse, Maurice, a French Trotter who came to us because his previous owners no longer wanted him. Honestly, he was incredibly stuck up and I did wonder how he would get on with Nero, but we felt sure they would sort themselves out.

The day came and Nero arrived. Maurice was running around as he knew there was someone new in that horse box. So the door opened, Nero ran across the field to Maurice, Maurice gave him an almighty kick and from then on, they had the strongest love/hate relationship ever!

They mostly hated each other, but if there was a situation they looked out for each other. I remember one night, very clearly, when we had the biggest thunderstorm ever. The lightning was so strong it was like someone had put a floodlight on the field. Julian and I went out to bring Maurice and Nero to their shelters. Julian had Maurice and I had Nero; the rain was pelting down and the lightning was terrifying. The whole time that Maurice was being led in front, looking back, checking on him. I saw then how much he really cared about Nero, he just did not like to show it!

When Maurice died, Nero stood and mourned for three days, just looking out across the mountains. It was one of the most heartbreaking things I have ever seen. He missed his friend.

From the moment I met him, I knew he was special. As I would sit and drink coffee, he would come over and rest his head on my shoulder. The connection was huge, his eyes were so deep and he loved you to whisper in his ear, telling him your secrets. Nothing was more comforting than hugging Nero and those who met him understood.

We shared so much. He was adorable, an absolute nightmare, but adorable. He hated other donkeys; in fact, he hated most of the other animals. He was special and therefore, no one came close to his expectations.

When we took him for walks around the mountain everyone admired him and he knew it. He was big, handsome and just incredible.

He would watch volunteers – calling to them to groom him. As they left, he would roll in the dust and call to the next one. He was the most groomed donkey in the world! He adored carrots and apples and would pretend to volunteers that he had not had one for days!

He was an incredibly strong donkey and if he was on a mission, he would run at full speed with his head held high – he really was donkey from Shrek. He would cause all kinds of disasters but to me, he did nothing wrong. He was perfect. There were many conversations that started with "your bloody donkey!"

The day he died I was in Africa. I actually felt my heart crumble. I had seen him the day before I left, the picture on the cover of this book was my last time with him. He had been in my life for six years. It seemed like everything was slipping away. I knew then the reason why I had put the book on hold. The universe was moving again. Now the book had an opportunity to not only help the animals at the Ridge, but others too. Even to the end, Nero was special.

I would hear him first thing in the morning and last thing at night and I still do. Nero will be in my heart forever and I hope, in the hearts of others too. I will sponsor donkeys around the world in his name, he will never be forgotten and honestly, he would love that his name was going worldwide. Perfectly fitting for the best donkey that ever walked on this earth.

LOVE YOU FOREVER MY MAN, FOREVER.
XX

THIS IS ANOTHER ONE OF THOSE RECIPES THAT VERY QUICKLY GROWS AND BEFORE YOU KNOW IT, YOU HAVE ENOUGH BALLS FOR EVERYONE, WHICH IS JUST THE WAY I LIKE IT.

POWER BALLS

YOU WILL NEED

Dates

Hazelnuts or any nuts or a mix, go mad, I prefer a mix, this way you get a different taste each time!

Sesame seeds

Sunflower seeds

Sultanas

Pumpkin seeds

Cup of raw oats

When it comes to quantities this is tricky, I really do just chuck the whole lot in a food processor and go from there, but use your dates as the base, this is the sticky element that brings it all together and always use the oats.

Coconut oil – again you do not really know how much until you have blitzed the other ingredients, you are going to use this to pull it all together.

It is good to point out here that this is a perfect time to use up all those odds and ends you may have in jars around the place. I think we all have them, so long as you use the dates and oats you can create some very interesting balls!

You will need a food processor for this; no two ways about it, you have to do it this way.

TO MAKE

1. Put everything, except the coconut oil, into a food processor and blitz. You want texture so smaller pieces, not a paste. When you are happy with the texture add coconut oil, not a great deal, just enough to give it a slight glaze; in this situation less is really more! If you do overdo the coconut oil just add some more nuts or seeds until you are happy with the results.

2. Now turn out onto a board and roll the mix in your hands, to the size of golf balls and set aside. You want something that is one or two bites, they are quite rich but they will give you the power burst you need if you are out and about and hungry or running late for breakfast, just keep some in an airtight tub ready for when you want them.

3. If you want to do something different, add desiccated coconut to the mix. Then melt some vegan chocolate and get some wooden kebab sticks (you can buy these very cheaply). Put one on the end of each stick and then dip in the chocolate; hold it until the chocolate stops dripping off and then place upright. When you have done them all, put them in the fridge. This is my version of a bounty bar! Naughty, but oh so nice!

JACOB

JACOB

Ahh Jacob, where to begin!

I first met Jacob whilst collecting Winnie Woo to come and live with us. The lady who owned Winnie Woo and Hamilton also fostered horses whilst they found new homes, and Jacob was one of these horses.

He was found tied to a tree; where he had been for two and half years. Jacob, along with his Mother who was pregnant at the time, was rescued and brought to safety.

I went over to him and gave him a hug and asked where he was going. I was told that he was heading to Easy Horse Care, the same rescue centre that Nero came from, but I whispered in his ear that one day, he would come and live with us.

I contacted them to ask if I could give Jacob a home. I was told that he was going to live there with them, but I never gave up because I just knew he would come to us.

A few months passed and the call came. Whilst Jacob was a lovely horse, he was not really settling into the sanctuary. I knew he would come.

He arrived and settled in immediately. Maurice found him disgusting but Jacob just loved to follow him around and Nero, well, Nero only had eyes for Maurice and tolerated Jacob.

He was, and is, a complete idiot but in a totally loveable way.

On the day that Maurice died he did something incredible, he rubbed himself along Maurice and it seemed he absorbed the spirit of Maurice. He grew up, whilst still maintaining his crazy behaviour and Nero; well, he took Jacob under his wing.

On the day we moved house, Jacob refused to get into the horse box until in the end, I whispered to Nero to show him how and Nero just walked into the box at which point Jacob followed.

Everything is a challenge for Jacob. Not people – more plastic bags, sprays, hose pipes – in fact, anything could possibly be dangerous (in his mind)!

Jacob has a wonderful connection with Julian. Jacob is his baby and often forgets his size, but if you needed to find Julian, he would be with Jacob.

XX

FILO WRAPS

YOU WILL NEED

The choices for the contents are limitless. Here are a few of my personal favourites.

- Leftover mac n cheese
- Cold potatoes with baked beans
  and vegan cheese
- Chinese stir fry
- Spaghetti in a pesto sauce
- Vegan cheese and cherry tomatoes
- Leftover tagine
- Leftover chili
- A mixture of pulses in a tomato sauce with a few nuts thrown in for texture.
- Stewed apple and custard (or any fruit)
- Poached pears stuffed with sultanas – just poach the pears in red wine, along with the sultanas so they soak up all the wine. Then, when cool, cut the pears in half and fill with the sultanas and then wrap in filo pastry. Reduce the poaching juice and use as a dressing.

TO MAKE

Firstly, I never ever make my own filo pastry, who would? Being vegan, it really is a thing to keep in your fridge; it lasts for ages!

You can make sweet or savoury versions of these. Again, go for what you have, use different spices and get creative. The secret is in the sauce you use, both within and on top. They cook quickly so it is better to have the contents precooked, or at least, something that just needs warming up so you can even make baked beans and cheese versions of these, just delicious and again, a great thing to make extra of to enjoy for a snack the next day.

1. I use two sheets of filo for each wrap, starting with one sheet and then double wrapping with another one. You can make them smaller, just go with how you like them.

2. To make them, just layout your filo pastry and then add your contents to the middle. Make one fold bringing the top down, bottom up and then bring the sides in. Continue rolling and then place rough edge facing down on a baking tray.

3. Once you have made your parcel, put onto a baking tray, drizzle with olive oil, for the savoury versions, and then sprinkle over sesame seeds and put into a hot oven for about 20 minutes or until they are golden and crispy.

4. With the sweet versions drizzle with water and then sprinkle sugar over before putting in the oven.

These are so quick and easy and you can literally fill them with just about anything, which makes choosing something to go with them so much easier. Rice,couscous, pasta all sorts and of course, a good salad always goes down well!

I HAVE NO IDEA WHY ANYONE BUYS HUMMUS, IT IS INCREDIBLY EASY TO MAKE AND YOU CAN CHANGE THE FLAVOURS TO CREATE YOUR OWN SPECIAL VARIETY. HUMMUS IS SO VERSATILE!

HUMMUS

YOU WILL NEED
This makes the base recipe

2 jars of cooked chickpeas, drained

2 cloves of fresh garlic

Zest and juice of one lemon
(You may want to add more juice at the end it really depends on the size of your lemon, go large!)

Tahini
If you do not have this no problem, just add a handful of sesame seeds.

Salt

Black Pepper

Paprika

Extra virgin olive oil

Hummus is for more than just dipping raw veg into. Use it in sandwiches, on jacket potatoes, on roasted veg or leftover roast potatoes by putting hummus on top, a drizzle of olive oil, a squeeze of lemon and then under the grill until it just browns, so delicious! Make a big batch to last a few days. Spread it on pitta bread, a bit of tomato, onion and oregano, drizzle with olive oil and black pepper and pop into the oven to warm through, delicious on its own or with soup! (Check out **Leeksoopdude**!)

You will need a food processor to get this smooth. You can also use a hand held blender, but for speed, invest in a processor.

TO MAKE

1. Put everything in the food processor except the oil and blend. Once you can see it is all broken down, start to add the oil whilst blending until you reach a smooth consistency. Taste it and adjust the seasoning as required and additional lemon juice if needed. Store in a covered dish in the fridge.

VARIATIONS

Try these additional ingredients at the blending stage to create different tastes, but not all at once! With the inclusion of nuts you will need a little less oil, so never add the oil until you have completed the first stage with all of these.

- Walnuts – Add a big handful to the mix before you add the oil.
- Black Olives – Using stoneless black olives, add a handful to the mix and blend before adding the oil.
- Roasted Red Pepper – You can use any you have left over from a previous dish or you can buy these ready prepared in a jar. They often come in olive oil, so drain first, but then you can use the oil at the end.
- Hazelnut – I really do suggest you roast these first, it makes all the difference and then just add them to the mix before you add the oil.
- Leftover Roasted Veg – Add to the mix, makes a fantastic hummus and is just brilliant on jacket potatoes!

 TIP

Mix hummus into mashed potatoes! You can then add nutritional yeast to the mix and roll into balls, deep fry them and then serve on a bed of green salad. Add lots of black pepper as you serve and a squeeze of lime or lemon juice too.

NOW THESE ARE GENIUS, THOUGH I SAY SO MYSELF! THE POINT IS TO MAKE TOO MANY — THIS WAY YOU HAVE LEFTOVERS WHICH CAN THEN BE SLICED TO USED AS A SANDWICH FILLING, OR EATEN COLD AS A SNACK, OR, IF YOU ARE MAKING A CASSEROLE THEY MAKE BRILLIANT DUMPLINGS!

FRITTERS

YOU WILL NEED

Almond milk
I always use a litre which makes loads but you can use half, or even quarter of this.

Flour
Any flour but you need enough to turn the milk into a batter.

Spices
Depending on what you are making add spices you like as well as plenty of salt and freshly milled black pepper. Sweetcorn Tinned is perfect.

Chickpeas
One jar or use any beans, however, lentils do not work very well! Drain
your chickpeas before adding.

Dried herbs
Again, go with your gut but I generally use oregano. Paprika and turmeric, not only adds flavour but gives a good colour too.

Baking Powder
I always over use this so if you want to be technical a Tablespoon, if you want to cook like me, a whole packet!

Additions
This is where you can use up odds and ends such as finely chopped courgette, onion or grated carrot. Remember not to have the pieces too big as they will not cook through. This is a good time, if you are in a rush, to use a bag of ready chopped mixed veg — quick and simple.

Fritters are the perfect food to make that just keeps on giving. These can easily be made gluten free too, just by using a gluten free option flour.

The main secret here is the milk you use. I always use almond milk as it is already much thicker than most other plant based milks, so it gives you a head start.

I also (surprise surprise) do not measure anything, but the process to create these – in other words, the order you put the ingredients into the bowl – is vital. You want to start with the batter and build from there.

What you put into your batter is up to you, so you could simply add finely sliced onions and some curry powder and create your own onion bhajis. You could also add finely chopped apples, some cloves and some maple syrup or sweetener of your choice to create a sweet version which can be served hot with ice cream. My point is, once you have the batter sorted, just go crazy with your ideas. This is a perfect recipe for using up all those odds and ends in your fridge and a little goes a long, long way!

TO MAKE

1. In a large bowl pour in your milk and add flour in small amounts whilst you stir until the batter is nice and thick. You want it to be the consistency of a thick custard.

2. Now, just add everything you want and stir. You want to have a mixture that is more filling than batter, so do not worry about adding too much; the more you add, the tastier it will be!

3. I now pop this into the fridge while I heat up the oil. Here you have two choices:

   - A deep fat fryer, turn it up to 165°C, that will produce big fluffy fritters.

   - Use a frying pan to create flatter versions. Before you do this, heat your oven to around 200°C so that whilst you're frying them, you can place them in after to keep them hot. It will also make them dry out a little to avoid a greasy fritter!

4. Take a large spoon and begin either adding to your deep fat fryer, leaving the basket in and carefully adding the batter; or spoon onto your frying pan. Do not get impatient here, cook a few at a time or you will end up with one, massive fritter!

Note: I also like to cook them quickly in the deep fat fryer to get the crust on them and then I put them into the oven to finish cooking. It is up to you how you cook them but I prefer to do it this way, then I can convince myself that this is not really a deep fried food!

I serve these with a salad and a spicy tomato sauce but you go with what you like best, garlic mayo, ketchup it is up to you . If you have made your fritters with Indian spices then you can always serve a cucumber and mint relish (which you will find in this book) which works really well! Serve them on rice or noodles too! Keep any left over in the fridge.

THE HERD

THE HORSES OF JACOBS RIDGE

When we first arrived at the Ridge, we arrived with Jacob and Nero. We were not planning to extend the herd as they seemed content with one another but, life takes you on twists and turns and now the Ridge has its own herd of horses with Jacob representing them all.

It was on a trip to a local farm that we discovered a breeder who was using his horses to breed and sell the foals, taking them away from their mothers after only a few weeks. This had been going on for years and the horses were all exhausted.

They were being fed oranges, lemons and straw so not only were they being emotionally tormented but they were also suffering from a lack of nutrition. They were bloated, tired and very sad. Most of them were kept in a tiny little paddock that fitted them in uncomfortably. Ankle high in their own waste and barely any shade. Jessie and one month old Woody were in a small area next to the others. This only gave

Jessie 8 meters (more or less) of space to move around in with the width being less meaning it was difficult for her to even turn around. Woody was always following her up and down which was limiting Jessie's movement even more.

The breeder then went on to say that he had got tired of looking after the horses and he had sold them to a local meat dealer, who was going to collect them all at the weekend.

The group sold included mares and foals and four of the mares were pregnant. Honestly, it just made us all feel sick. We offered there and then to buy them. We were not sure how we were going to do it, but, there was no way these beautiful animals could be sold for meat and let the breeder end their lives in the most horrendous manner possible.

The breeder said no, they had been sold, however if the buyer did not turn up on Sunday morning, then we could buy them.

The buyer never arrived and at 12.01 pm we were there ready to take them home.

Whilst we were standing and negotiating terms, another horse raised his head above a wall trying to get our attention. We asked who this horse was, to which the reply was "Oh, you can take him as well if you want". So we did. That's how he got his name, Spirit. We named them all on how we felt about them; from the energy they gave off. We found out later that Spirit is actually Wilhelmina's son but since he was taken away from her way to soon they lost their bond. I don't think they even remember each other.

We walked Jessie, her one month old boy Woody, Verity with her three month old boy Merlin, Grace, Lucy, Wilhelmina and Spirit.

Within this herd, Verity, Lucy, Wilhelmina and Grace were all pregnant. Sadly, Grace lost her foal. Stress, poor diet and apart from that, it became very clear that she had been very badly treated and even now she has major trust issues, but there is something about Grace that just makes you want to hug her (at your own risk). She has a deep, deep beauty that, despite everything, shines through.

The remaining foals went full term and were born at the Ridge. They have only known love and they know it! Lucy is mother to Maggie, Wilhelmina is mother to Misty and Verity is mother to Zor. When Verity came to us she already had three month old Merlin, she had Zor a bit later on. Shows you how much they were being bred. You will never see Zor or Merlin too far away from their loving Mum. Same goes for Misty and Maggie.

The rescue of eight horses turned into 11 horses in the herd. It has been a long, long journey to get them back to health but now they stand as a beautiful example of the right environment, the right food and above all, love and respect.

The herd are a testament to a huge amount of work and their gift in return is the love they give back and the connection they make with everyone who visits the Ridge.

There is a big olive tree in the middle of their paddock. It is a place where you can sit whilst the horses gather around you. It gives you time to think, to focus. Every time one horse, or sometimes more, will come and be with you to help you through your personal thoughts. Horses are incredibly spiritual, so you just have to open up and let them in. They truly are healing and beautiful.

Their message is love, loyalty and respect. At least, that is the message I get from them.

XX

NOW, I HAVE EATEN A FEW VEGAN BURGERS IN RESTAURANTS, THEY WERE EITHER TOO THIN, IN FACT I HAD TO CHECK THEY WERE EVEN THERE, OR SO BLAND IT WAS LIKE EATING CARDBOARD. THERE IS NO REASON IN THE WORLD WHY A VEGAN BURGER SHOULD NOT BE BIG, THICK AND JUICY. SO HERE IS THE RECIPE FOR THE FAMOUS VFP BURGER.

THE VFP BURGER

YOU WILL NEED
for 4 burgers

1 jar of ready cooked lentils

1 jar of ready cooked chickpeas (you can use just chickpeas or just lentils if you prefer. Just go with what you have)

2 cloves finely chopped garlic

Heaped Tablespoon of dried oregano

Level tablespoon of paprika (heaped if you want it spicy)

½ a teaspoon of chili flakes unless you like the heat, then add more

Teaspoon of salt and ten turns of the pepper mill or a teaspoon of black pepper

2 or 3 Tablespoons Nutritional yeast

Splash of soya sauce

Squirt of ketchup

Mustard (I use Dijon but you can use any mustard) two teaspoons

1 Tablespoon Liquid Smoke (optional)

Handful of pumpkin seeds

Handful of sesame seeds

Flour Any type

Olive oil for frying / baking

 TIP

If you double up the recipe, you can then use the other half to create vegan "meat" balls which you can then serve on spaghetti with our spicy tomato sauce, this avoids extra cooking for the next day, make your life easy!

TO MAKE

1. Drain the lentils but not the chickpeas. Put everything into a large bowl, including the chickpeas and their juice. This is the secret to binding all the ingredients together. (If you are using different beans just use the juice from those!)

2. Mix it all together and add enough flour to bind it all together.

3. It does not need to be a solid lump but it needs to be a texture that is almost holding together.

4. Now put in the fridge whilst you prep for cooking.

5. Heat your oven to 250 degrees. Now, using the pan you are going to put in the oven, put a good slug of oil into the pan and put on the hob to eat through, medium heat, we are looking to just seal the burgers. I use metal rings to measure out the burgers but if not, you can just divide the mixture into four rounds. You can use extra flour to bring them together.

6. Now put into the pan and fry gently until they are brown on each side. Now put the pan into the oven for around 20 minutes, turning halfway through, until cooked and hot right through. Serve in a bun with all the usual additions and of course, chips!

7. "Meatballs" If you have made extra, then take the remaining ingredients and roll into golf ball sizes, put on floured plate, cover and put in the fridge ready for tomorrow. When you are ready, just shallow fry in olive oil until brown all over then add a couple of teaspoons of ready made curry powder to the pan until you can smell the spices (you can use anything here, just experiment) and then add a jar of sieved tomatoes and heat through. Serve on spaghetti, rice or couscous with a salad. Any left overs pop into a piece of fresh bread with a big splodge of vegan mayonnaise and mustard, delicious!

You can make these gluten free very easily just change the flour and check the labels on your soya sauce.

VARIATIONS

Falafel Burger

Use chickpeas only but add a Tablespoon of dried mint.

Ground cumin, teaspoon

Ground coriander, teaspoon

Serve the burgers in a pita bun with cucumber and mint relish and a ton of fresh salad leaves.

Mushroom and Leek Burger

Chop up some mushrooms and leeks, I use about a handful of mushroom and a couple of leeks and sauté until soft. Season and then add to your bean mix.

Chili Burger

Make your burgers with kidney beans and add a little extra flaked chillies to the mix and a little secret, add a big spoonful of Marmite to the mix too. Serve with all the trimmings!

THIS IS A FAMILY FAVOURITE. THE MIX OF CREAMY, SMOOTH MASHED POTATO WITH A DEEP, RICH LENTIL MIX IS JUST THE PERFECT HOME FOOD. ALL I SERVE WITH THIS IS A MIXTURE OF FRESH, STEAMED VEGETABLES. IT IS ALL IT NEEDS.

SHEPHERD'S PIE

YOU WILL NEED

For the mash

4 large potatoes, peeled and cut into quarters

Olive oil

Almond milk, or any plant based milk. Don't worry about how much; you will see as you mash

Salt

Freshly milled black pepper

Freshly grated nutmeg, about ten up and downs on your grater!

For the base

2 jars of lentils

2 jars of sieved tomatoes

2 red onions, finely chopped

2 handfuls of mushrooms, finely chopped (I chop these very finely so my children do not notice)

4 cloves of garlic finely chopped

4 carrots finely chopped or grated

2 parsnips finely chopped or grated

2 leeks, very finely sliced

1 courgette, grated.

1 cup full of frozen peas

2 vegetable stock cubes

2 dessert spoons of dried oregano

1 dessert spoon of dried thyme

1 large dessert spoon of mustard

2 glasses of red wine

1 Tablespoon of Marmite

2 teaspoons of paprika

1 pinch of chili flakes

½ a cup of nutritional yeast

Salt and freshly milled black pepper

If you want to change this to a cottage pie you just layer the top with sliced, pre-cooked potatoes. Drizzle with olive oil, salt, black pepper and oregano and cook in the same way, but for me... mashed every time!

I always use lentils for the base as it gives the perfect consistency. You want the mix to be creamy – not too runny and not too solid, as you want some of the juices to soak into the potato whilst it is in the oven.

TO MAKE

1. In a large pan filled with salted water, boil your potatoes until soft and then drain. Now mash, add a glug of olive oil, your milk and mix together. Add enough milk until it is smooth and then add your black pepper and nutmeg. Mix and set to one side.

2. In a large pan, add a glug of olive oil, add your onions, a big pinch of salt and just cook until the onions have softened a little. Now add all your other vegetables, herbs and spices and give it a good mix. Do not add the nutritional yeast yet.

3. Now add your tomatoes, wine, lentils and mix again. Top up with water, enough to cover it all, give it a good mix and then let it simmer for about 30 minutes or until all the vegetables are soft. Set to one side. Now mix in your nutritional yeast. If it still seems a little runny, add a bit more along with additional salt and black pepper to taste.

4. Now put the lentil mix into a baking tray and top with your mashed potato. Pop into a hot oven, 200°C, until you see it bubbling around the edges. You can leave it a bit longer to get a crunchier topping if you prefer.

Garnish

I like to serve with portobello mushrooms that have been roasted in olive oil, salt, pepper and garlic. I just pop them in the oven when I put the shepherds pie in, delicious, and of course, great if you blitz to create the base for something else. Actually, if you make loads It makes the most awesome mushroom pate. Just blitz with a couple of handfuls of pitted black olives and add nutritional yeast and there you have it.

A real favourite in our house and one you can make in advance.

 TIP

Make extra mashed potato if you want, because you can use when it is completely cold to create croquette potatoes. Just add some vegan cheese, pre-cooked veg like mushrooms or peas, extra seasoning, shape, dip in chickpea water, then in breadcrumbs and fry until golden.

← THIS IS FREDDIE.

I LOVE CHILI, SO COMFORTING AND WITH A GLASS OF BEER IT IS JUST PERFECT. IT HAS A HOMELY FEEL TO IT. YOUR HOME FILLS WITH THE MOST AMAZING SMELLS AS IT SLOW COOKS ON YOUR STOVE. IT HAS THE WONDERFUL EFFECT OF HAVING PEOPLE NATURALLY GATHER TO THE KITCHEN TO SEE WHAT IS COOKING, SO THERE IS NO NEED TO YELL WHEN DINNER IS READY. BELIEVE ME, THEY WILL ALL BE WAITING.

CHILI SIN CARNE

YOU WILL NEED

This sounds like a ton of things but once you have made this once or twice you will probably never look at this recipe again.

A good slug of olive oil, enough to cover the bottom of your big pan

2 red onions chopped, no need to go super fine on this, you want rustic

2 red peppers, sliced

4 carrots, grated

2 sticks of celery, finely chopped (even if you hate celery, please use this)

2 large glasses of red wine

1 Tablespoon of Marmite

4 squares of dark chocolate

6 cloves of garlic, finely chopped

2 vegetable stock cubes or two large dessert spoons of vegetable granules

1 or 2 Tablespoons of chili powder, depending on how hot you want it

3 teaspoons of ground cumin

2 teaspoons of smoked paprika

1 Tablespoon of dried oregano

2 bay leaves

2 jars of sieved tomatoes

2 jars of chopped tomatoes

4 jars of kidney beans (change for other beans if you prefer)

1 large bunch of fresh coriander

Zest and juice of 2 limes

Water

This is a dish that works really well the next day and is perfect for using in the filo wraps or stuffed peppers, so don't worry if at anytime it starts to feel like you are cooking for 100 people. It freezes well, so look upon it as a bit of batch baking!

Some people say they hate kidney beans. If you really cannot stand them, just replace them with something else, but not lentils. This needs a rustic feel about it, so think bigger beans. I also like to throw in a couple of tins of aduki beans too. (Just a side note – aduki beans are awesome little things, they actually collect up fat from your body and, lets just keep this pleasant since it is a cookbook, dispose of it for you. Add them cold to your salads too – delicious.)

Think flavour all the way through this, think slow cook, think depth, think rich, think awesome.

Give yourself time with this, it is the sort of thing you prepare on a Saturday lunch time to enjoy Saturday evening, the longer you can leave it the better. Whilst the ingredient list looks horrendous, it actually is very quick to prepare and then you can just set it to one side to simmer, slow and long, as you get on with other things.

TO MAKE

1. Start with a nice big pan!

2. In your pan pour olive oil, enough to cover the bottom and then add your chopped vegetables along with a very big pinch of salt. Now just cook until they are soft and then add all your dried herbs and spices. Cook again for about a minute – basically you want the spices to release their flavours.

3. Now add your jars of tomatoes, beans, wine, Marmite and chocolate. Chop the fresh coriander, saving some for garnish. Give it all a mix and then add water to ensure that everything is covered and mix again.

4. Bring it up to the boil. Now reduce it down to a slow simmer, as low as you can go, and just leave it. Check every now and then to give a stir and add a little more water if needed.

5. After an hour turn it off and leave it. When you are ready to eat the chili you can heat it through again and then add the lime juice and scatter the fresh coriander over the top.

I like to serve this on a jacket potato, fried tortilla chips which I sprinkle with a mix of salt and paprika, guacamole and a huge, crisp salad, but go with what you love most to serve it with.

 TIP

So, having collected all your ingredients, whilst you are measuring out your spices for the first time, get an empty jar and create your own chili spice mix so the next time you only need to reach for one jar.

THE PIGS

☞ THIS IS OREO

THE PIGS

Pigs are my personal passion ever since I met my first pig, face to face, at the age of five. They are just so special, so beautiful and I love people meeting the pigs and seeing that each one is different with their own personalities, likes and dislikes in fact, just their own people.

Pigs have the intelligence of a three year old, so when you find yourself standing in a group of pigs just see them like a group of children. Some will be paying attention, some will just wander off, some will only want to be with their best friends, others will have a fight and well, you get the picture!

Contrary to belief, pigs are very clean animals, they do not want to live in filth, they need a good diet. Yes, pigs will eat anything but that does not mean it will do them any good. Pigs have the same digestive system as humans do so when feeding the pigs you have to ask yourself, would you eat this? If the answer is no, then it is not good enough for the pigs.

Just like humans, pigs have their own tastes. For example, Elvis likes his oranges peeled and prepared for him, others like to have the orange whole, roll on it to release the juice and then bite into it. The more you get to know them the more you understand just how special they are.

At the Ridge there are lots of pigs, but there are the main characters who shine through and who visitors often connect with such as Oreo, Wilbur, Bella, Lila, Twinkle, Fergie of course Winnie and Elvis, Peggy, Carmella, Bill and Ben, Derek, in fact, too many to mention but the important thing is that each one is special.

Some were born at the Ridge but most have been rescued from various situations. Some from happy homes where they have just outgrown their surrounds, others from disgusting situations, some found abandoned on the streets. Just like a class of children, each has their own story to tell.

The main message that the pigs give is simply this "Friends not food." How anyone can eat pigs after spending time with them I have no idea, how any sanctuary can be anything but vegan is beyond me but through spending time with the pigs at the Ridge it helps people to at least consider vegan then that's wonderful.

XX

I'VE SPENT A GREAT DEAL OF TIME WATCHING PEOPLE PREPARE PAELLA AND TO BE HONEST, THEY SEEMED TO MAKE A GREAT BIG DEAL OF IT WHEN ACTUALLY, IT IS VERY SIMPLE. HOWEVER – YOU DO REALLY NEED TO HAVE A PAELLA DISH AND COOK ON GAS OR OPEN FLAME TO REALLY GET THIS AUTHENTIC.

PAELLA

YOU WILL NEED

Rice

This will depend on the size of your dish. I have a huge dish so I use 8 cups of rice, but for a normal size I am going to estimate you will need two or three cups. Remember, you are going to be adding more ingredients and double the amount of stock to rice so think about that when you start, a paella can very quickly start coming over the sides!

Vegetables

1 onion, finely sliced

1 red and one green pepper, sliced

1 jar of roasted red peppers

1 whole head of garlic

Celery – not everyone likes this so it is optional

1 jar of chickpeas, drained

A bunch of flat leaf parsley or whatever you can get, but make sure it's fresh

One or two lemons, quartered

1 jar of sieved tomatoes – get the best you can

Spices

Salt

Freshly Milled Black Pepper

Paella spice mix – I make a big jar of this and then I only have to spoon out what I need. It is made primarily of paprika, turmeric, (equal amounts) dried oregano, about a quarter of the amount of paprika and a large Tablespoon of chili flakes. Mix and store in a jar. For an average sized pan, go for a dessert spoon of the mix.

Stock

You are going to need double the amount and maybe a tiny bit more than the amount of rice you use. However, I make mine with white wine and a vegetable stock cube. It really does make all the difference.

First and foremost, paella should be moist and firm. At the bottom it should have *socarrat* – this is the crunchy layer of rice that forms on the bottom of the pan and it is the bit everyone argues over. You will never get this in any other pan or without using gas to cook. Trying to make paella in a frying pan on an electric stove will give you something completely different and not as good, as it should be more of a one pot rice dish.

Secondly, get the correct rice. You cannot do this with any other rice except paella rice. Now here in Spain we can obviously get this very easily and I use Calasparra rice, grown locally. When shopping make sure you get the correct rice – rice for risotto is designed to be creamy when cooked which is not the results you are looking for.

Thirdly, and this is very important, the stock you use will have a huge effect on the final flavour as will the spices you put in.

A word of warning, never use mushrooms in a paella if you are planning to use the next day, it will turn grey!

TO MAKE

1. Firstly, get everything ready – it makes life much easier. Prepare your stock so it is hot and ready to use and have all your ingredients at hand; then it really is a very quick process to prepare.

2. Heat the oil in your pan, add the onion and cook until soft, not brown. Next, add your spices and stir around for a few minutes. Add your vegetables, whole head of garlic (just remove the paper bits from the outside) and chickpeas too. If you need a little more oil, now is the time to add it. Stir and then add your rice, stir again to ensure all the rice is coated in the oil and spices. Now add your stock; remember that for each cup of rice you will need two cups of stock. Now mix through and then add your jar of sieved tomatoes and mix again.

3. Make sure your whole garlic is in the centre of the paella dish and wait for it to come to the boil.

4. Now reduce it down to a low heat and cover with tin foil, being sure it is sealed.

5. Golden rule, just leave it. Do not mix, do not do anything to it for at least 20 minutes. Then check, very carefully as the contents will be very hot under the foil, to taste the rice. If it is cooked through then switch off the heat and just leave it, if not, let it carry on for a bit longer.

6. I like to let mine sit for at least 10 minutes before serving and then I unwrap and sprinkle over the parsley and then lay the lemon wedges around the outside to make it look pretty.

7. Serve with a huge salad and loads of warm bread. Paella is meant to have a bit of fresh lemon juice squeezed over it, so once you have served it on a plate don't forget to add the Spanish touch with lemon wedges, it makes a big difference to the taste. This makes a brilliant filling for the filo wraps so any left over, you know what to do with it!

THE MAIN SECRET TO MY PIZZA IS THE CRUST. SO OFTEN THE CRUST IS JUST A SIMPLE DOUGH BASE BUT WITH A LITTLE IMAGINATION YOU CAN CREATE A WONDERFUL BASE THAT WILL HAVE PEOPLE ASKING WHY IT TASTES SO GOOD.

PIZZA

YOU WILL NEED

For the dough:

Half a kilo of flour – You can use bread flour but since this is not easily found here I tend to use any old flour and it works

25g pack of fresh yeast or a teaspoon of dried yeast

1 Tablespoon of sugar

Half a litre of warm water

A glug of olive oil

A very big pinch of salt

If you are using fresh yeast then add this to the water along with the sugar and stir, leave until it froths up and then it is ready to use.

Now, for the extra ingredients:

A handful of sunflower seeds

A couple of Tablespoons of sesame seeds

Dried oregano – Just tip about a Tablespoon in

Dried garlic – Roughly a couple of teaspoons

Dried onion – Roughly a couple of teaspoons

Freshly milled black pepper

 TIP

No time to make dough? If you are in a rush you can, of course, use pitta bread and do the same thing!

Pizzas are brilliant because you can pretty much make anything! Once you have the base you can very easily put together a calzone, which means you can create individual ones for each person's personal taste and, even better, they make perfect snacks for the next day, so always just prepare one to keep ready for the next day by saving a little of the dough from the pizza.

TO MAKE

1. Put all the dry ingredients into a bowl or mixer and then add the olive oil. Now make a well in the middle and start adding the yeast mix or, if you are using dry yeast add this to the dry ingredients and then start adding the warm water.

2. Bring it all together until you have a ball. You may need a little more, or less, of the water so just add a little at a time until you reach the consistency you want.

3. Now turn out onto a floured board and knead until it feels soft, like a puppy's belly, and then it is ready. Set to one side and cover.

4. Now, what to put on top?

   The secret to a good pizza is not to go too mad with the toppings. Keep the ingredients to just a few really good ones, so be creative and make your own signature pizza, but for the sauce, here is my suggestion.

   I use a jar of sieved tomatoes, always buy the best you can, the taste is so much better than the cheaper versions. If I have leftover pesto I add this too. If you use the pesto there is no need to add dried oregano; if not, then be liberal with it. You can also add some dried chili spice if you fancy a kick! Now add your grated vegan cheese or if you do not have this then you can always add equal amounts of nutritional yeast and ground almonds, just add away.

   ### Here are a few suggestions for your topping:

Fresh, thinly sliced tomato	Sweetcorn
Olives (I put these whole around the edge as not everyone likes them!)	Thinly sliced onions (I always use spring onions but they are massive out here!)
Thinly sliced leftover potato	Peppers
Thinly sliced courgette	Mushroom and so I could go on but you get the idea
Asparagus, just lay these on the top	

5. Roll out your dough nice and thin, unless you particularly like deep pan. Then put onto a baking tray or baking paper. I prefer to use the paper as the pizzas seem to cook better when you use just the sheets in your oven shelf, that said, if you are going to do this, put the pizza onto the paper on a board before you begin with the toppings, it makes it so much easier to handle! Then just add all your topping choices.

6. Now, over the top of your pizza add a few more sunflower seeds, salt, black pepper and a little more dried oregano and then drizzle the whole thing with olive oil. Do not go nuts with this, just a light coating; you want flavour not a greasy pizza!

7. Put into a 250°C hot oven and depending on the thickness of your dough, serve when the crust is golden and the toppings are hot. I like to throw fresh rocket on my pizzas before serving for a little extra peppery seasoning.

NOW THIS IS MY SIGNATURE DISH. I JUST LOVE ITALIAN FOOD, I LOVE THEIR APPROACH, ONLY FRESH INGREDIENTS, I LOVE THAT THEY PUT SO MUCH PASSION INTO EVERYTHING THEY EAT, I LOVE THAT THEY SEE FOOD AS AN OCCASION NOT JUST SOMETHING TO KEEP YOU BREATHING.

LASAGNE & BOLOGNESE

YOU WILL NEED

Glug of olive oil

2 red onions, finely chopped

Pack of mushrooms, finely chopped

3 cloves of garlic, finely chopped

1 courgette
You can cube this but I normally grate it so my children do not notice!

4 carrots, grated

2 tins of sieved tomatoes

2 glasses of red wine

2 jars of lentils

2 vegetable stock cubes

1 dessert spoon of Marmite

1 dessert spoon of dried oregano

1 bunch of fresh basil
This is the best option but if you cannot get it, a dessert spoon of dried (but do try to get fresh)

A cup of nutritional yeast

Water

FOR THE WHITE SAUCE

A good glug of olive oil

2 tablespoons of flour

Salt and freshly milled black pepper

1 glass of white wine

1 heaped teaspoon of mustard (any will be fine)

1 Tablespoon of dried oregano

About a litre of plant based milk, I use almond

½ a cup of nutritional yeast

½ a cup of ground almonds

 TIP

I like to serve it with a few leaves of fresh basil on the top, but you should certainly serve it with hot pesto bread (see page 136) and lashings of delicious fresh salad.

I have tried loads of "vegan" lasagnes and I have yet to be impressed. There is no reason at all why a vegan lasagne should not be better than one made with just animals, in fact, I have served this to hardened meat eaters who never even noticed that it was vegan!

So, I do use pre made lasagne sheets when I am in a rush, but you can make your own if you wish, but for this recipe I am using ready made, but everything else is from scratch. Take your time with this and if you make it the day before it is actually better, it gives the lasagne time to really settle and for all the flavours to merge together. So here it is, my vegan lasagne!

This makes one big lasagne, enough for six people, but anything left over can be portioned and popped into the freezer so for those busy evenings you can just take a piece out in the morning and in the evening, warm through and it's ready.

I use one large pack of vegan lasagne sheets for this, but I always buy two packs just in case I need an extra few sheets!

TO MAKE THE SAUCE

1. In a large pan add a big glug of olive oil, enough to cover the bottom of the pan and add your onions and a teaspoon of salt. Cook until soft then add your garlic. Mix and then add the rest of your vegetables.

2. Mix around and then add everything except the nutritional yeast. Top up with water, give it a good mix and then it just simmer quietly while you prepare the sauce. Keep giving it a little stir and after about 30 minutes check the seasoning and add more salt and pepper if required. You are looking for this to reduce down a little, not too liquidy. At the very end mix through the nutritional yeast and set to one side ready to prepare your lasagne.

What you now have is the sauce for your lasagne, or... you have your bolognese sauce! Two in one.

TO MAKE WHITE SAUCE

3. In a pan add a good glug of olive oil, I usually count to five, and then just gently heat. Now add your flour to the oil and mix. Then slowly add the white wine to the flour and oil and then add your milk, slowly, until it is all smooth. If it gets lumpy, don't panic – just get a whisk out and give it a whisk through.

4. Now add your mustard, oregano, salt and pepper. Keep stirring until it thickens. Next add your nutritional yeast and ground almonds. Taste and season again if needed. If it gets too thick, just add a little more milk until you have a thick, creamy, white, cheesy sauce. Set to one side.

TO ASSEMBLE

In your lasagne dish, add a layer of the lasagne sauce and layer the pasta sheets over. Repeat until you have three layers of lasagne sauce and three layers of pasta sheets, finishing with the pasta sheets. Now pour over the white sauce covering everything. Give it a little shake and then sprinkle with a little more dried oregano. Then pop into a hot oven, 200°C, for about 40 minutes or until the pasta is soft. Just put a knife through and check it is all soft.

If you're going to eat it straight away, when you take it out of the oven leave it to 'set' for about 15 minutes. It makes it a little bit easier to serve.

Lasagne

Bolognese

THIS IS ONE OF MY PERSONAL FAVOURITES, IT JUST BURSTS WITH FLAVOUR, COLOUR AND OF COURSE THE AROMA IS OUT OF THIS WORLD. EVEN BETTER, IT REALLY IS A CASE OF CHUCKING IT ALL TOGETHER AND LEAVING IT ON A VERY LOW HEAT TO DO ITS THING.

TAGINE

YOU WILL NEED
for a large tagine

1 onion finely sliced

6 carrots, peeled but not c hopped, keep them whole.

1 large courgette cut into chunks

Handful of cherry tomatoes

Roughly 8 each of dried dates and apricots (very important to use these)

1 Tablespoon of harissa spice or paste

2 desert spoons of peanut butter

1 whole head of garlic

1 Tablespoon of dried oregano

Bunch of fresh coriander

1 jar of sieved tomatoes, get the best you can, it really adds depth to the flavour

Salt and freshly milled black pepper

1 jar of chickpeas

1 red chili finely chopped (optional or use less if you do not want to keep it mild)

1 vegetable stock cube or granules.

Water to cover

Handful of nuts, I normally use cashews or you can used flaked almonds too, just use what you have it just gives another texture in the final dish

Now, you can do this in a pan, of course, but the tagine is a wonderful thing to have in your kitchen, it really does help in the cooking process. If you are going to buy one, get a metal one, the kind that would be used in an authentic way. You do not want one that is just pretty – you know the sort I mean – more to make your kitchen look pretty than actually have a use.

The main thing to remember is not to overfill your tagine, it is very easy to get carried away and then spend the next few hours mopping up the juices as they overflow, trust me on this!

TO MAKE

1. In your tagine, or pan, head up a glug of oil and then add your onions and just cook gently until slightly soft.

2. Now add your spice, or paste, and mix through.

3. Next add your courgettes, dates and apricots, nuts, chili (if using) and mix through.

4. Add your oregano, salt and black pepper.

5. Now mix in the whole head of garlic. Add your sieved tomatoes and stock cube. Break it up a little as you put it in. Mix everything through. Throw in a handful of cherry tomatoes, chopped coriander (including stalks) and peanut butter.

6. Now cover everything with water and give it a good mix. Now, lay your carrots on the top, in a ring. Bring it up to bubbling and then turn down the temperature to low. Put the lid on and leave it for at least an hour before you look at it again.

7. You will know it is ready when the carrots are soft. The joy of this dish is you can literally just leave it doing its thing whilst you get on with other stuff.

8. Once the dish is ready I like to throw on top fresh spinach and a few sesame seeds before serving. Put the lid back on and the spinach will have wilted before you reach the table. In the picture I have topped the tagine with roasted slices of sweet potato, beetroot and some shoots. A handful of chopped coriander works just as well.

9. Serve with couscous (page 84) and a bunch of friends!

← THIS IS MEGAN.

THIS IS SUCH A SIMPLE DISH TO MAKE, BUT BE WARNED, COUSCOUS CAN BE VERY, VERY BLAND, SO SEASON AND ADD LOTS OF THINGS TO REALLY BRING IT ALIVE.

COUSCOUS (FOR MEGAN)

YOU WILL NEED

2 cups of couscous
(enough for 4 people)

1 teaspoon of salt

1 teaspoon of black pepper

1 teaspoon of chili flakes

1 dessert spoon of oregano

A handful of sesame seeds

Lime zest and the juice of a lime

Olive oil

6 English spring onions
(or 1 Spanish spring onion,
they're huge!), finely chopped

6 sundried tomatoes, finely
chopped (get the ones in oil so
they are already soft)

A few golden sultanas (optional)

A slug of rose water (optional)

The great thing is that it is brilliant hot, brilliant cold and very easy to pop in a tub and have a ready made lunch for the next day.

TO MAKE

1. In a bowl, add your couscous, now add salt, black pepper, dried chili flakes, dried oregano, sesame seeds, lime zest, the juice of a lime (you can use lemon here or try with orange too or all at once!) a good slug of olive oil, some finely chopped spring onions, a few golden sultanas (optional but I really like them) a slug of rose water (optional) finely chopped sundried tomatoes (get the ones in oil so they are already soft). I also like to add some sieved tomato at this stage too, without actually measuring it out I would say about a ladle full if that helps! Mix it all up.

2. Now boil a kettle and pour over just enough water to cover everything and about quarter of inch above that, mix, put a lid on it and leave it to soak up all the water. Then lift the lid, mix with a fork, taste and add any additional seasoning like more salt and pepper or another squeeze of lemon juice.

3. I also like to add, if in season, pomegranate seeds, flaked almonds, fresh coriander and mint chopped up and a quick flick over with pumpkin seed oil, or sesame seed oil whichever you have.

4. Ready to serve.

 TIP

Leftover cous cous can also be used to stuff peppers, tomatoes, all manner of things, so never throw it away. It also works if you mix it with chickpeas; keep the liquid and use this as a binder until you can form patties. You can then fry them and serve with avocado and salad or within a bap. Great take away snack too, and particularly good stuffed in a pitta bread with a big blog of hummus. In short, a very quick and very versatile ingredient to have in your store cupboard.

THIS IS THE DISH THAT EVERYONE LOVES – EVERYONE REQUESTS IT! ONE YOUNG LADY, MENTIONING NO NAMES, (BUT LET'S CALL HER KAYLEIGH!) MANAGED TO EAT SIX FULL PLATES, ONE AFTER THE OTHER!

VEGAN MAC 'N' CHEESE

YOU WILL NEED

Macaroni – I use one cup per person

1 vegetable stock cube

Cheese Sauce

1 litre of almond milk
Always use almond milk, it is already much thicker than other plant milks so it gives you a head start.

A few good glugs of olive oil

3 Tablespoons of flour

4 cloves of garlic, finely chopped

Dried oregano, if I was measuring I would say around a desert spoon

1 teaspoon of mustard

1 cup of nutritional yeast

Two or three big handfuls of vegan grated cheese (if you do not have this, it's no problem. The nutritional yeast will be okay on its own, but grated cheese does make a difference)

About half a glass of white wine

Salt and freshly milled black pepper

TO MAKE

1. Firstly, cook the macaroni. I always use a vegetable stock cube as it adds flavour to the pasta. When it is almost ready, soft but still a bit firm, drain the pasta and pour into your big dish.

2. Heat the oven to 200°C.

3. In a big pan heat up the oil on a medium heat. Gently fry the chopped garlic, then add your flour to mix together to form a paste.

4. Add the wine slowly and then just cook for a minute. Then slowly add the milk, if you get lumps just whisk them out.

5. As it starts to thicken add all the other ingredients and mix through, let it just come to the boil and then pour over the macaroni. Give it a mix and then put into a big oven proof dish and then into the oven until it bubbles.

That's it, super easy and very delicious. I often add a little extra something to go on top just before serving such as asparagus cooked in lemon, garlic, salt and black pepper.

Note: If your sauce is too thick, just add more milk. If it is not thick enough then add more nutritional yeast. You want it to be able to coat all the pasta so avoid making anything too thick.

 TIP

Additions – If you want to add a little more flavour, before you add the flour to the oil add finely chopped leeks and cook until they are just soft then add the garlic. Cook through and then continue as before.

TAPAS IS HUGE IN SPAIN AND THE IDEA IS BRILLIANT. RATHER THAN HAVING A SINGLE DISH OF SOMETHING YOU CAN ORDER A SELECTION, WHICH IS BROUGHT TO THE TABLE, WITH A SMALL PLATE, A FORK EACH, SOME FRESH BREAD AND OF COURSE, OLIVE OIL.

TAPAS

Tapas is also a brilliant way to use up odds and ends in your fridge and get creative with your spice cupboard. Create little bowls of delicious tasters; they look fantastic, taste incredible and it is always a talking point when people start to ask what each dish is.

Here are just a few ideas, but the principle of a tapas is just small bowls of delicious things to share over a drink, so once you get going you come up with loads of ideas!

Chickpea and Cashews

In a flat pan which has a lid, (I use a wok for this), add a glug of olive oil, count to about two seconds and then add a half teaspoon of paprika, a pinch of dried chilli, a teaspoon of oregano and a teaspoon of curry powder. Let it sizzle for about 30 seconds, then carefully add a drained tin of chickpeas and a handful of cashew nuts. Give them all a good mix and then turn the heat right down and put the lid on. You do this because the chickpeas can explode! After about ten minutes give them another mix through and set to one side. You can heat them back up when you need them or serve them cold, equally delicious just make sure you toss them in salt and freshly milled black pepper before serving.

Spicy Roast Cauliflower

Heat your oven to 200°C and then take your cauliflower (you can use a whole one or just a half whatever you have), break it down into bite size pieces and add to a baking tray. Next, roughly chop a red onion and add to the tray.

Now chop a courgette into about half inch slices and add to the tray. Obviously, you can add whatever you have; for example a cubed aubergine works equally well. Next add a whole garlic bulb with the top sliced off. Drizzle the whole lot with olive oil and give a good mix. Now add salt, black pepper, paprika, cumin power and onion power, about a teaspoon of each. Give it another good mix and put into the oven until the cauliflower is cooked. I normally give this a mix through about every 20 minutes. You can always do this and then turn it into a delicious soup by blitzing and then adding enough vegetable stock to get it to your desired consistency. Also makes a great sauce if you blitz it too, so versatile! (You can also do this with broccoli or both at the same time!)

Slow Cooked Mushrooms

I hear so often how people do not like mushrooms because of the texture, but the secret here is to take your time and let them cook very slowly. This way all the moisture evaporates and you end up with the tastiest mushrooms in the world. The big secret to this dish is patience.

In a flat pan, add a good slug of olive oil and once warm add your mushrooms. You can use a selection of types but just make sure they are chopped or sliced, we want all the moisture out. At this point, add harissa paste or dried spice or whatever you have to hand along with some dried garlic flakes. Next throw in a tin of drained, pitted, black olives. Add salt and pepper, a couple of glugs of soy sauce and then turn it down super low and leave them. Every now

and then give them a stir. Serve in a bowl with the whole garlic so people can pick out the garlic cloves, and sprinkle with chopped fresh parsley. These are delicious and many a "non-mushroom eater" have enjoyed them!

Roasted lemon, garlic and rosemary potatoes

This recipe can obviously be used for full-sized potatoes to serve with any dish, but for tapas you need to cut the potatoes into small pieces. Remember, tapas is eaten with forks, not knives and forks, so you are always looking at bite size pieces when preparing.

Heat your oven to 200°C and then chop your potatoes, (how many depends on how big your potatoes are, but work on a medium sized potato for two. I never bother peeling them). Chop into bite size pieces and then add to your baking tray along with a lemon cut in half, a few sprigs of fresh rosemary (or dried) and a whole head of garlic with the top sliced off. Next, drizzle in olive oil and give it all a good toss, you want the potatoes to be coated in olive oil but not swimming in it. Sprinkle everything with salt and put into your hot oven, give them a turn now and then, and when they are crunchy and beautiful they are ready. Before serving, squeeze the roasted lemon over the potatoes and serve with the garlic as it is so people can pick out the roasted cloves.

These are delicious. If on the off chance you have any left over, make them into a potato salad the next day. Just mix with a vegan mayo, chopped spring onions and seasoning and you have another awesome side dish!

Rich Tomato Sauce

This is something you need that can be spooned onto plates and tapas can be dipped into the spicy sauce.

In a saucepan, add a good glug of olive oil and then add about a tablespoon of curry powder. Give it a quick mix through. As it heats up you'll smell the spices, when that happens move the pan off the heat.

Now add a tin of good quality sieved tomatoes; again, one tin for about two people. Then add fresh coriander, including the stalks and mix through. Add water, just fill one of the tins and add this to the mix along with salt and freshly milled black pepper. Put back on the heat, bring up to a simmer and then leave it simmer for about 20 minutes. At this point I normally add a tin of coconut milk, just because it gives it a creamy finish, but it is not essential. After 20 minutes add about a cup full of nutritional yeast and give it a good mix through. Let it simmer for about 10 minutes more and then take it off the heat. You can add to the spiciness of this dish with a splash of tabasco sauce if you wish. The more you make this, the more you start to create your own blend of sauce. This is one of those recipes where you can make extra and then the following day you have the basic starting point for a curry. Saves a huge amount of time in a busy week. Serve this in a bowl so people can spoon it onto their plates or over their potatoes.

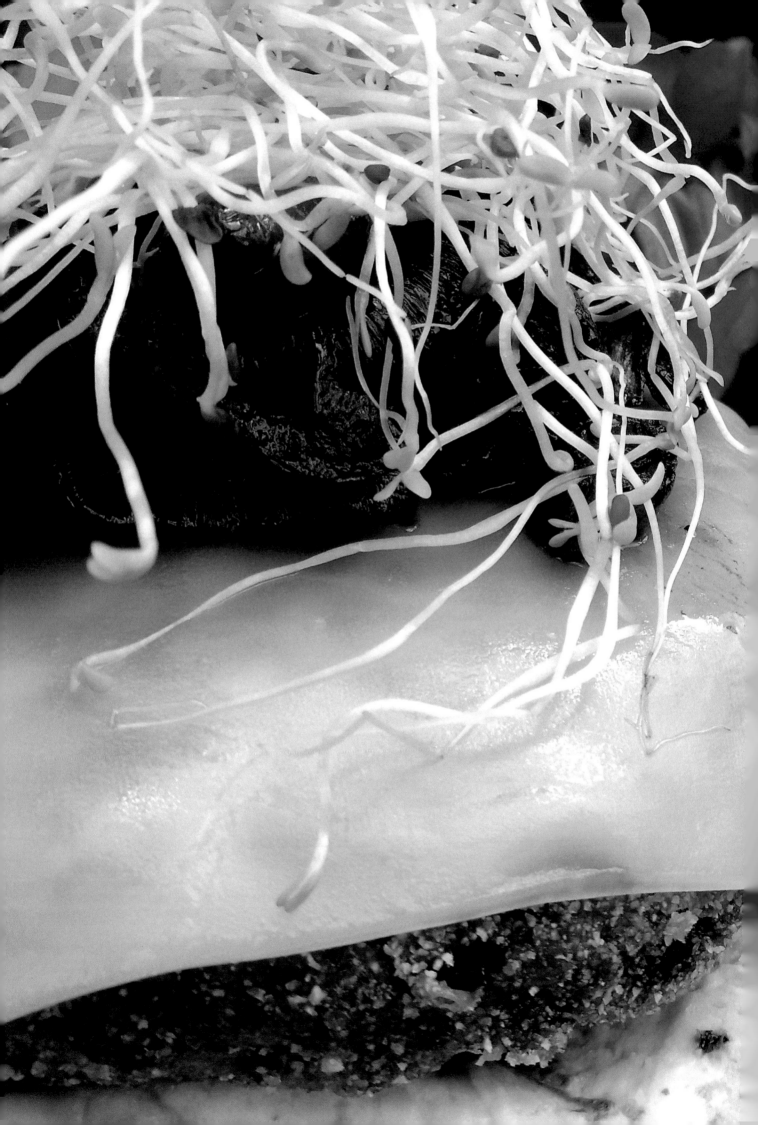

THIS IS ONE OF MY PERSONAL FAVOURITES BECAUSE IT GIVES YOU A HOST OF DIFFERENT TASTES AND TEXTURES. FIND A BAKERY THAT SELLS VEGAN BREAD AND GO FOR SOMETHING BROWN AND NUTTY, IT REALLY MAKES A DIFFERENCE TO THE FINISHED DISH.

BRUSCHETTA

This is also a dish where again, you can use bits and pieces out of your fridge and left overs too. Nothing wrong with a blob of leftover curry or tagine on one of the pieces!

Your bread

This really does call for good quality bread, do not try this with that horrific plastic stuff in a bag. Get an uncut loaf and slice yourself a good thick piece, at least half an inch thick, about a fingernail deep. I normally cut three for each person but you can decide how much you want to eat!

Now, you can rub a piece of fresh garlic over each piece, but normally just use garlic oil, drizzle it over the bread and then set it to one side while the grill is heating up. Then just toast until golden and it is ready to add your toppings!

Pictured on this page, we have:

Roasted Cherry Tomatoes

Easy to do these and make extra. You can use them in so many things, like putting them into your tagine, adding them to a curry, adding them couscous, squashed and spread on toast... the list goes on!

Heat your oven to 200°C. Add olive oil to a baking tray, enough to coat the bottom of your tray, then add your cherry tomatoes whole along with four cloves of garlic, chopped roughly, salt, pepper and a drizzle of balsamic vinegar. Roast until soft. Serve on the bread with lots of the garlic and a drizzle of the oil which will be infused with all the flavours.

Garlic Mushrooms

I use button mushrooms for this, handful for each person. I just cut them in half, put them into a baking tray and then add a clove of garlic per person, half a glass of white wine and some fresh coriander. Drizzle with oil and then mix it all up and pop into the oven until the mushrooms are cooked through. Serve on the bread with a squeeze of fresh lemon or lime juice.

Asparagus & Fresh Spinach

This takes moments and I eat this on its own when asparagus is in season. Just prepare the asparagus by holding each piece in your fingers and then bend it. It will snap naturally where the woody part ends and the delicious part remains. Do this with all of them and then add to a frying pan with just a little oil, a squeeze of lemon, salt and lots of black pepper. Cook it for a few minutes. On the bread add a handful of raw spinach and then put the asparagus on top pouring over the oil and lemon from the pan.

Avocado and Black Olives

Peel your avocado and either mash or slice and add a little lemon juice, lots of black pepper and a sprinkle of chili flakes. Then just slice up a couple of black olives and put on top.

Just delicious!

ELVIS

LONG LIVE THE KING!

Elvis came along, with Mia and Pixie, through a friend of Hamilton's Mum. Hammy was responsible for so many animals that have found their way to us. The day these three arrived, I instantly connected and fell in love with Elvis.

The three of them had been rescued from another situation and the family that took them on could not keep them anymore, they asked us if we could help. The three of them came out of the back of the van, Mia and Pixie went off to explore but Elvis was clearly upset. He loved the lady who looked after him and he did not understand what was happening.

As the van drove away, he ran after her and sat by the gate, confused and upset. My heart melted.

He has the most incredible eyes and you could see he was sad, so I set about making sure he had everything he needed, and more. Slowly, he came round and we connected. That connection is so strong.

We would spend time just sitting and being together, I would rub his belly, he would sleep, occasionally opening one eye to check what was going on around him and then, back to sleep.

When we relocated to the Ridge, he was the first to introduce himself to the neighbours, but not quite in the way that he should have done!

Whilst working in the field, we had a visit from the local police who had received a complaint about our pigs. Now, to put this into perspective; we had been living at the Ridge for about a week, so things were still very much "work in progress". Many did not really understand why on earth anyone would keep pigs and not eat them, even now, people still ask if they can buy one claiming to want them as a pet which, clearly, is not the case. When we explain that they are part of our family they just look at us like we are insane, but at the end of the day that's their problem!

So, back to the police. It turned out that a "large pig" had been seen eating the neighbour's beans and the land owner was incredibly angry. I instantly jumped to the defence of the pigs and mentioned that the whole area was full of wild pigs and how on earth did he know it was our pigs? He produced a photograph and there, with a mouth full of beans with a big smile on his face was Elvis! After much discussion it was agreed that this would not happen again and that we were very sorry. He did do it again and again, but then, no one knew – until now – so no harm done! To be honest, it was such a beautiful picture that I really wanted to ask for a copy but I thought that may have been pushing my luck!

Elvis loves his photograph being taken and in 2015 he became the face of most of the promotional work for people to come to the Ridge. I loved taking photos of him; playing in the straw, just being around him. We trust each other and that is an incredibly special bond to have with an animal.

Elvis is the person I would work with to demonstrate to others just how special pigs are. People would see his personality, his special ways and start to make the connection between what they have been eating to him being a living, breathing being.

I remember one boy who came to stay with us in 2015 who was only five years old. Arun was in the situation of having a mum who was vegan and a dad who was a meat eater. Obviously at five this was confusing and he had not yet made the connection with animals but I knew that over the course of a week, he would make that connection.

I asked him if he liked curry to which he replied, "Yes, I like chicken curry!", his poor mum looked mortified but I said don't worry, just hold on a minute. I went and got Susan, a chicken who lived with us. I put her into the arms of Arun and said, "This is Susan. She is a chicken."

Arun loved her, stroking her and I saw him make the connection. Nothing else needed to be said. Connecting people with the reality of their food is so important.

Over the week Arun spent loads of time with Elvis, being with him, sharing his mud bath and just hanging out like two friends would. Elvis was incredibly giving to Arun, he genuinely loved him. It was wonderful to see this small boy with a huge pig just being together, no barriers, no issues, just being together.

On the day that Arun left he turned to me and said "I am not going to eat Elvis anymore". It was beautiful. Elvis has converted so many people to being vegan, they all have in their own way, but Elvis, he really is the star of the show and he knows it. He has a swagger, he can be demanding, he can be downright rude to some people but to me, Elvis is the King of Jacobs Ridge and one of the most beautiful images is to see him sleeping under his fig tree as the sun sets on another beautiful day.

Long Live The King
XX

THE PICTURE PRETTY MUCH EXPLAINS THIS RECIPE BUT FOR ME, WHEN IT COMES TO PORTION CONTROL, THIS IS IDEAL. ONE ROLL EACH, A FEW SIDES AND YOU HAVE A VERY FULL AND HEARTY MEAL.

STUFFED BUNS

YOU WILL NEED

Vegan bread buns

Any fillings, such as

- Chili
- Curry
- Bolognese sauce

You can buy vegan bread buns in most places now, but if I see some good ones I buy a load and pop them in the freezer. This way, you can prepare one or 50 at any time; all you need is the filling.

TO MAKE

1. To prepare them, just cut the tops off and pull out all the bread from inside and set to one side.

2. Leave the tops to one side and pop just the rolls into a hot oven for about 10 minutes, just to dry them out a little so when you add the filling they do not end up with soggy bottoms! (No one wants a soggy bottom)

3. Then fill the buns with anything such as chili, curry, bolognese sauce (all the recipes are in this book). I have even used leftover shepherd's pie on a particularly cold night. Once filled, put the lid on top and drizzle with olive oil and sea salt and pop into the oven until hot through.

If I do not have quite enough to fill the rolls then I add a little extra stock to my left overs and mix through the bread I pulled from the rolls to fill them out. If you are not going to use the bread then freeze it, you can use it for breadcrumbs for something else.

Easy and always a winner!

NUT ROAST IS ONE OF THOSE DISHES THAT, TO BE HONEST, WILL TASTE EVEN BETTER IF YOU CAN MAKE IT THE DAY BEFORE, BUT WILL STILL BE GREAT IF IT'S MADE THE SAME DAY IT'S SERVED,

NUT ROAST & VEGGIE WELLIE

YOU WILL NEED

This sounds like a ton of ingredients but it is super easy to make and once you have made it a few times you will no longer even look at this recipe, it will be in your head!

4 jars of ready cooked lentils

1 jar of sieved tomato

1 or 2 roasted peppers
(Buy these ready done in a tin)

Bag of fresh spinach, chopped

4 carrots, grated
(I often buy a bag of ready chopped veg to throw into this too, whatever is easier for you just make sure that you chop up the veg nice and small)

1 courgette, grated

2 red onions, finely sliced

2 handfuls of mushrooms, chopped into small pieces

4 cloves of garlic, finely chopped

1 Tablespoon of dried oregano

1 Tablespoon of dried thyme

1 Tablespoon of paprika

1 cup of nutritional yeast (optional)

Handful of nuts, chopped
I normally use almonds because they are cheaper here, but any nuts will be fine. Chop them up into small pieces.

Half handful of seeds
It can be a mix of pumpkin, sesame
or sunflower or all of one.

Salt and pepper

One vegetable stock cube

Olive oil

Flour to bind. You can easily make this recipe gluten free.

You will need a loaf tin for this recipe and I would suggest lining it. I use a paper loaf case, which works really well. If your nut roast is to be served on the day, allow yourself enough time to let it stand and "set".

I use lentils for this but you can use a mix of lentils and other pulses, so do not be put off if you do not have enough lentils in your larder. I always use pre cooked; it's so much easier and to be honest, if you are anything like me, much better for portion control too!

This recipe will make two nut roasts, so you can freeze the second one and then use it to make a Veggie Wellie at a later date. It just saves a huge amount of time in the kitchen. I have put the extra details below.

You will need two small loaf tins or if you only have a big one, no problem, make it as one. It will need a little longer in the oven and just cut it in half if you want to freeze the other half.

TO MAKE

1. Heat a big saucepan along with enough oil to cover the bottom. Add your chopped onions with a teaspoon of salt and cook until the onions are just going soft. Then add the other vegetables and the garlic to the mix, adding a little more oil if needed. Add all your spices and the vegetable stock cube, broken up. Cook until the vegetables are softened. Take off the heat.

2. Now add your pulses, sieved tomato, nuts, seeds, nutritional yeast if you are using it and give it all a good mix. Add more salt and lots of freshly milled black pepper. Now add enough flour to bring it all together.

3. Set it aside for about 30 minutes and now turn on your oven to 200°C.

4. After 30 minutes have a look at your mix, you should be able to lift it out with a large spoon rather than pour it, so if it still seems too runny add more flour but remember always when adding flour to a dish to add more seasoning as plain flour tastes of nothing! Once you are happy then you are ready to pop it into the tins.

5. Put the lining in your tins and then divide the nut roast mixture between the two or into one big one. Stand the tins in a large oven tray with water in the bottom and then pop into the oven for about an hour. What you are looking for is when you put your finger on the top of the roast it feels solid.

6. Once cooked take out of the oven and let it stand for about 20 minutes before you take it out and slice it. Longer wait time is better, but 20 minutes should be enough. Serve with a sauce or gravy along with a good selection of veg.

7. Nut roast is also delicious cold and I have used left overs to put into a casserole; just chopping any left overs into pieces and adding to my pot.

Veggie Wellie

Using a pre-cooked nut roast, this is super easy to do. You can buy vegan flaky pastry now, which makes life a whole lot easier, so I use this. Roll it out, spread it with a thin layer of English mustard, then a layer of cooked mushroom. Place the cooked nut roast on the top and roll it up.

Brush with water and then sprinkle with sesame seeds. This is always delicious served on a bed of slow cooked spicy red cabbage!

Nut Roast

Veggie Wellie

THERE ARE A MILLION CURRY OPTIONS OUT THERE, BUT FOR ME, A CREAMY, DELICIOUS CURRY LOADED WITH PULSES, VEGETABLES AND SPICES, SERVED WITH A CREAMY COCONUT RICE HAS TO BE THE BEST THING EVER.

CURRY

YOU WILL NEED

Coconut oil – You can use olive oil but I really think this makes a difference. A Tablespoon should be enough.

2 red onions

1 courgette, cubed

1 red pepper, cut into small pieces

Grated fresh ginger, about a dessert spoon full

Four carrots, either in small pieces or grated

Four cloves of garlic, chopped

Bag of fresh spinach

Handful of golden sultanas (optional)

1 apple, chopped into cubes

2 tins of sieved tomatoes

2 tins of pulses
I like to mix; so chickpeas and butter beans for example

2 tins of coconut milk

Dessert spoon of Marmite (Yes, really – try it!)

2 teaspoons of tamarind paste

1 vegetable stock cube.

2 large teaspoons of peanut butter

1 handful of cashews (You can use peanuts too)

1 large bunch of fresh coriander

SPICES

Option One

Dessert spoon of curry paste or powder of your choice.

Option Two

2 teaspoons each of cumin, coriander and turmeric and 1 teaspoon of chilli powder

Now, this is a bit of generic recipe, but this is a great base and from here you can build. The cucumber and mint dip works incredibly well with this, just saying!

The next thing I want to mention here is that this looks like a load of spices, but, the best thing to do is to create your own jar of "curry spice" by making your own mix. That way, when you want to knock up a quick curry, you do not have to mess about with loads of jars, just one big spoonful of your mix. It also means you can create the exact spice you want, the right heat, the right depth.

I also love potatoes in curry, but always use pre-cooked potatoes, this way they absorb the flavour of the curry whereas if they are raw, they end up a bit hard and bland, so, do not go out of your way to cook potatoes but any left over, into the curry they go!

Also, never be ashamed to buy a curry paste and use that instead of loads of different spices, what is important is what you put in it. Curry is an incredible source of iron so by the time you have added your pulses and vegetables, you have a really nutritious meal and since curry always tastes better the second time around, make extra to freeze. Freeze in food bags and then when you fancy a curry, take out in the morning so that by the time you get home in the evening all you have to do is cook some rice and warm up the curry! Saves loads of time and leftovers are perfect for the stuffed buns or the wraps. So, now to whip up a brilliant curry!

The curry in my picture has an onion bhajee on top which is using the same batter for the fritters only I added curry powder to the mix. It needs to be like wallpaper paste, stirred in with thinly sliced onion and then just dropped spoonfuls into hot oil. You can do it with cauliflower and broccoli, too.

TO MAKE

1. Super easy! Heat the oil and fry the onions and spices. Once your kitchen is filled with the aroma of curry, add all your other vegetables (except the spinach), the nuts, the fruit, the stock cube and give it all a good mix to be sure everything is covered.

2. Now add your sieved tomatoes and stir. Add your pulses and then enough water to cover it all.

3. Now mix in your coconut milk, Marmite, tamarind and half the fresh coriander; use the stalk end and save most of the tops until near the end. Add salt and lots of freshly milled black pepper.

4. Bring it to the boil and then reduce to a simmer until everything is cooked. Just before serving tip in the spinach, which will wilt very quickly and mix through. Now add the remaining fresh coriander and it is ready to serve.

See recipes for Coconut Rice and Cauliflower Rice on page 112.

RICE IS SO VERSATILE. GO OUTSIDE YOUR COMFORT ZONE AND BUY DIFFERENT TYPES.

I always throw in a bag of rice with my shopping and, sadly, get very excited if I find something new! This obsession, however, does mean that I always have something in the larder that I can throw together to make a meal, so there is method in my madness.

Just changing your usual rice in a recipe can change the whole meal. Each type of rice has its own taste and texture. For me personally, a favourite in my kitchen is Basmati. It adds a more subtle, nutty taste and smell to a dish than your usual long grain rice (which has its place) but when it comes to taste, Basmati every time. That said, there are some recipes where you need to use the correct rice, such as for paella or risotto when you use arborio rice to achieve perfect results.

The two types of rice I like to keep on my shelves are wild rice and black rice. Both look stunning on a plate and taste delicious.

Experiment with different kinds of rice and remember, one cup of rice to two cups of water or stock. That is enough for two people. If you have a rice cooker, you can just throw it all in there and forget all about it whilst you are doing something else. Perfect!

COCONUT RICE

YOU WILL NEED

Golden rule:

1 cup of rice, 2 cups of liquid
One cup is enough for two people

TO MAKE

In a pot, add your rice and then add one cup water, one cup coconut milk, any leftover coconut milk can go into the curry. Add salt and then bring to the boil. Let it boil for about five minutes then turn off the heat, put a lid on. Leave it for about 20 minutes and you will have perfect fluffy rice every time. If you want yellow rice, just add a teaspoon of turmeric to the water before bringing to the boil.

CAULIFLOWER RICE

YOU WILL NEED

1 cauliflower

Peanut or olive oil

Salt

Black pepper

TO MAKE

This is so easy and so tasty. Just break up the florets of the cauliflower and put into a food processor. Blitz and hey presto, cauliflower rice. The secret is in the cooking. In a large pan, I use a wok, add a little oil, I use peanut oil but again olive oil is fine, and add salt and pepper and then just heat through and there you have it, cauliflower rice. You can change the taste by adding the zest of a lemon or orange, or experiment with different spices. In fact, just experiment!

POPPY

PRINCESS POPPY

Princess Poppy was one of the first animals we rescued. She came from a goat farm where she was destined to become a Sunday dinner at only a few weeks old, so we took her home.

Poppy was only 6 weeks old when she came to live with us, just in time for Megan's 11th birthday. There was instantly a bond between them.

Megan learnt very quickly that you cannot house train a goat and that it really was not a good idea to have her sleep in your bed with you. As the bedding and mattress were thrown away, I think she finally understood that I knew what I was talking about!

The day we bought her home, Megan was holding her in her arms and Julian said, "Put her down, she will be fine!" The next hour involved running around, falling down and basically attempting to catch this very fast little lady!

Poppy grew up with dogs and in her mind she was not a goat. In fact, if she met other goats she actually looked disgusted.

Poppy was so posh. I always felt she was the lady who did the flowers in the local church and sat around drinking tea. She really should have worn a straw hat every day, although she probably would have eaten it.

She would go for walks with the dogs and loved being with Megan, just curled up on her whilst she was tickled behind her ears.

Poppy connected with so many people at the Ridge. She was so gentle and loved treats although, unlike most goats, she was actually quite fussy.

She loved figs, fig leaves, banana peel (but not bananas, they smelt funny), not carrots (they smelt funny), loved hard corn, flowers (just taken not offered), vegetable patches, trees, olive trees, apricot trees... in fact, any trees!

Now, Princess Poppy had so many runs built for her and she would stay for a few weeks and then break out and come to the house as if to say, "No, not for me thank you!" On one occasion she found her own house – an empty tent. Everyone was searching for Poppy, who had gone missing, until she was finally found asleep in one of the tents, oblivious to the stress she had caused everyone. That was Poppy; a law unto herself.

The day Princess Poppy died was awful. She had been with us for 7 years. To think where she could have been, how short her life would have been, it is wonderful to look back on Princess Poppy with nothing but smiles and know that she touched so many people by being on this planet.

XX

NOW, I LOVE RISOTTO. HOWEVER, I DO NOT ALWAYS HAVE THE TIME, OR PATIENCE, TO STAND AND STIR A RISOTTO. THIS METHOD MAKES IT SUPER EASY!

OVEN BAKED RISOTTO

YOU WILL NEED

1 large onion, chopped

2 cloves of garlic, chopped

A good slug of olive oil

Risotto rice, 1 cup for two people

1 glass of white wine, drink half and save the rest for the risotto!

2 handfuls of cherry tomatoes

A bunch of fresh basil
(You can used dried oregano if you prefer) Save some of this for serving

The juice of half a lemon

1 cup of frozen peas

Nutritional yeast

Vegetable stock, twice as much as the rice you use

Lots of freshly milled black pepper

A main benefit of oven baked risotto is you can make much more without any stress. I always make extra as it works really well as a stuffing in peppers, in a wrap or just fried up with the addition of some Chinese spice, soya sauce and a few vegetables to create a whole different flavour.

This method is so easy so do try it!

TO MAKE

1. Heat your oven to 200°C.

2. In a frying pan, add a good glug of olive oil and add your chopped onion and a good pinch of salt. Once this has started to soften add the chopped garlic. Now, carefully pour the wine into the mix and cook for about a minute more. Mix in your rice and make sure its all coated. Add the cherry tomatoes, the fresh basil, the lemon juice and the peas. Add more salt and lots of freshly milled black pepper.

3. Now pour into a baking tray suitable for the quantity of rice you have.

4. Pop into your hot oven for around 20 minutes or until the rice is cooked through. Then served drizzled with extra olive oil, the nutritional yeast and the remaining fresh basil. I also like to dot around some super spicy sauce, just for an extra dimension along with a crisp salad.

Delicious and without all the fuss. You can change the taste of the risotto by changing just one or two of the ingredients, you can swap the basil for mint to create a mint and pea version or you can cook the onions in curry powder, add a few nuts, some dried fruit, fresh coriander and some cooked vegetables. Then, split the vegetable stock with half coconut milk to create a simple biryani.

Once you have the basics the options are limitless!

NOW, THIS RECIPE WAS INSPIRED BY THE LITTLE FAMILY AND TO BE HONEST, HAS BEEN A TRIUMPH! IT ALL CAME ABOUT WITH THE PROCESS OF WORKING OUT WHAT WORDS WERE BEING SAID IN A VERY STRONG GLASWEGIAN ACCENT AND THE RESULT WAS A DELICIOUS SOUP!

LEEK SOUP DUDE

YOU WILL NEED
For a large pan of soup

6 large leeks, finely chopped

6 medium sized potatoes, cut into chunks

2 cloves of garlic, crushed

Almond milk, ½ a litre or ½ a box

Enough cider to cover everything

Oregano, around 2 teaspoons

Paprika, around 2 teaspoons

1 Tablespoon of Marmite

1 teaspoon of mace

1 bay leaf

1 teaspoon of mustard seeds

1 teaspoon of turmeric

Equal mixes of ground almonds and nutritional yeast, about half a cup of each

Salt

Freshly milled black pepper

1 teaspoon of mustard

Glug of olive oil

Now, I am not really into "baby food" soups so I keep this quite chunky, but go with what you prefer. If you prefer something smooth then just blitz at the end but really, it is super good as a chunky, wholesome meal as it is, of course, with some good, warm, crusty bread and lashings of freshly milled black pepper.

Again, I do tend to just wing it and I hope this all makes sense, but I do strongly recommend you try this!

So, how to make Leek Soup Dude…

TO MAKE

1. Simply fry the leeks in the olive oil with the crushed garlic until transparent. Then, add your potatoes and mix through. Add salt and pepper at this stage along with your oregano.

2. Now, add the milk and mix through. Once it is warmed through, add the yeast and almonds, once again give it a good mix. Now cover with cider, you want it to be just above the mix.

3. Stir in a teaspoon of mustard and leave to cook, gently, until the potatoes are soft. This works really well the next day so if you are planning ahead, this is a great thing to prepare.

4. Once the potatoes are soft the soup is ready. If it is looking at bit thick at any stage just add a little more cider. Taste and see if it needs any more seasoning and it is ready to serve, just another twist of freshly milled black pepper and you are good to go or you can add all the trimmings and serve with fresh, warm bread – absolutely essential!

Topping Optional (but maybe for special occasions or if you want to spoil yourself)

Fried rice noodles, crispy mint and rocket and slithers of fried leeks and finally, scattered with crunchy toasted cashews.

HAMILTON

Hamilton was responsible for so many key family members at the Ridge. Through him I found Winnie Woo, Nero, Elvis, Mia, Pixie, Little Red, Prospero and many other beautiful Pigs and Jacob.

This was another of those strange situations where the Universe moves and starts you on a journey you never planned or expected but where you just sit back and enjoy the ride.

I remember, very clearly, talking to Julian saying how you always saw puppies needing a home but never a piglet. I think he was listening, but someone else was.

The following week in a free local magazine, in the classified section "Homes needed for piglets". The universe is very powerful, so much so that Freddie has become a little nervous that I have put up pictures of some of the wild animals we saw in Africa, I think he feels sure that he will open the front door and they will all be standing there!

I contacted the lady, Lorraine, who said that all the piglets had been homed, I was so disappointed but she asked me if I would be interested in taking an adult male pig as her dogs did not like him and she did not want him shut in a pen all day. I agreed. So off we all went to pick him up armed with a dog carrier.

Upon arrival it was clear that a dog carrier, or a car, was not going to be enough to bring this big lad home!

I fell in love with him at first sight. He was running around making the noise of a Harley Davidson, which explains the wild hog thing, rolling in water and generally being, well, Hamlet. Julian looked mortified but I knew he would learn to love him and he did.

We went home again, borrowed a mini bus and got a bigger box and returned for him. When we returned two of the piglets had not been collected so we took them too. We came home and put them in the back area of the garden whilst we finished their run. In the space of about five minutes Hamlet had emptied every flower pot, broken just about everything and finally he collapsed in a heap. He never really changed from that mindset.

He loved people, a little too much sometimes, most were terrified of him but he would never have hurt a soul. He would stand by the front gate and people would call from there, afraid to come in, but you would call him and he would race over.

He loved oranges but only peeled, he loved pasta but only with a sauce, he hated mushroom and only liked cooked

carrots but no, he was not fussy he just knew what he liked.

He was incredibly strong and incredibly smelly but I loved him. If he ever got out of his run he would come straight to the house and knock on the front door, or rather, attempt to push the door in.

He was a total nightmare but I loved him, my beautiful Hamilton.

XX

I LOVE THESE – EASY PORTION CONTROL, EASY TO MAKE. GREAT TO MAKE THE DAY BEFORE TO SAVE TIME AND ANY THAT ARE LEFT OVER CAN ALL BE BLITZED UP TO MAKE AN AWESOME PIZZA BASE SAUCE!

STUFFED PEPPERS

When choosing your peppers for this, find one that have four bobbles on the bottom, these are sweeter and if you want them to stand up with the tops on, find those which are flatter, if, however you do not have time to play with the peppers in the market or supermarket, just cut them in half like these! If you are buying them particularly for this recipe then I would suggest getting a selection of colours just because, for me, they look pretty!

I have given you a selection of ideas to fill your peppers but the prep is important, you do not want a "hard" exterior, you want them to be soft without being soggy, so here is how I prepare them.

Cut them how you want to use them, so if you are planning to stand them up, cut off the tops and set to one side. Then clean out all the seeds and the bitter yellow "bits" from inside, give them a rinse and they are done. Do the same if you are cutting in half.

Now put them in a pan of water, bring to the boil and then turn off the heat and let them sit there for about 10 minutes. This just softens them and helps them cook better, in my opinion, when they go into the oven.

Lift them out and drain on kitchen roll.

NOW THE STUFFING!

This has to be the perfect little pot to use up leftovers such as curry, paella, chili, in fact anything really. What is important is the moisture element in these, you do not want a dried out pepper with a dried out filling.

Put the peppers into a baking tray and then drizzle the insides with olive oil, salt and freshly milled black pepper. You can also add at this point some dried garlic salt too.

Now fill your pots up with your filling. I like to add a few extra bits too. So you can always sprinkle over some additional nuts and seeds to give it a bit of crunch and then finish off with a drizzle of olive oil.

Put them into a hot oven for about 15 minutes. When you take them out, sprinkle over each one some nutritional yeast, another quick drizzle of olive oil and back in the oven for another ten minutes.

Whilst these are roasting I also like to add to the tray a few cherry tomatoes and a lemon cut in half which can then be squeezed over the peppers. The oil that is in the tray, along with the tomatoes is delicious, so mop it up with fresh bread, yum!

 **TIP**

Whenever you are roasting something like this, use the space in the baking tray to use up any odd bits and bobs in your fridge. You can always add around the tray chunks of courgette, aubergine, fennel, carrots, parsnips etc. These can then be used in a couscous salad or blitzed with ready cooked lentils, paprika and nutritional yeast, to create a delicious pâté that can be spread on pita bread and baked. Always look for opportunities to take advantage of the time you have in the kitchen.

STUFFED SQUASH

YOU WILL NEED

1 small squash per serving (one per person), or

1 large squash

Leftovers for stuffing

How many squash really depends on how many people and how big your squash are, when I am buying these I try to look for the smaller ones so you can prepare one for each person. However, if you can only find a huge option, no problem, you just have to serve a piece of the squash rather than the whole thing.

Also can I say, never throw the seeds away from your squash, they are delicious roasted and eaten as they are or sprinkled over salad, I have put how to do this at the bottom – so much nutrition ends up in the bin! I was just about to go on about making stock, however, stopped myself just in time!

So, to make stuffed squash...

TO MAKE

1. First and foremost give your squash a wash and leave it whole. Put a couple of holes into the squash, this will stop it from exploding. Cook in salted boiling water until just soft. Then set aside to cool.

2. Once cool enough to handle, either carefully cut off the top for individual or lengthways for a whole version.

3. Heat your oven to 200°C.

4. Scoop out the seeds and set to one side. Then scoop out the flesh leaving about a quarter of an inch behind to hold the squash together. No need for a ruler or anything here; you just want to make space for the stuffing but keep the squash in one piece.

NOW, STUFFING...

5. This is a perfect opportunity to use up leftovers so I like to stuff these with all sorts. Before I add anything to the squash, I like to add a good drizzle of olive oil, some garlic salt, salt and freshly milled black pepper. Then fill them up with something like left over risotto or chili. After, top with a big spoonful of nutritional yeast, a little fresh lemon juice and olive oil, put the lid on once done.

6. Place on a baking tray. I tend to use a smaller baking dish for this so I can "squeeze" them in and keep them upright. Then give them another drizzle of olive oil and a good sprinkle of salt.

7. Pop in the oven until they are starting to "wrinkle" a little. At this point they should be cooked, normally about 20 minutes is enough.

8. Serve with a big fresh salad and depending on what is on the inside of your squash, you can serve with couscous, rice or anything else you fancy. This is another dish that I always try to make one or two extra from because you can always blitz these to make the most incredible squash pate, which you can spread on hot pitta bread or as a pizza topping.

Roasted Squash Seeds

Give them a quick rinse, then mix with a little oil and salt. Pop them into a hot oven for about 15 to 20 minutes, or until golden then take them out. Go easy – they can "pop". Delicious on just about everything, including with sandwiches. If you have the room plant them, they need hardly any attention and from one seed you can get quite a few squash. They will sit in your larder quite happily for months.

BARNEY

THE RIDGE DOGS

There are actually four dogs who live at the Ridge. Three actually "live" there and one, Eyebrows, lives with me because, let's just say she is a bad influence on the others!

Each one has a story to tell, so let us begin with

DAISY DUKE

When Julian and I first got together, after a while we got a dog, George, a chocolate labrador, who stayed with us for 17 ½ years. He went through everything we did. He was there to meet Megan and Freddie when we bought them home from the hospital and he was always one of the family. He will always be special because he was our first dog. It also gave us an intense love of labradors.

When I was approached about a labrador that needed a home, at first I was unsure. We have to be so careful about dogs at the Ridge, as not all dogs are friendly towards other animals such as cats, pigs and birds so I had to be sure that this dog was really a labrador. It turned out she was.

Now, previously to this, Freddie had a dog, Ben who he adored. He'd had Ben since he was a puppy. He was found abandoned by the rubbish bins. He loved this dog. Sadly, Ben was poisoned by someone. Freddie was with him when he died and it broke his heart. I felt that Daisy had been brought to us for Freddie, so we said we would take her.

Daisy was in a pound, dumped there by her previous owners who said she was too difficult to walk. She was 8 months old. I think the reality was Daisy had grown out of her tiny puppy stage. Like all labradors, she needed attention. If they don't get it, they destroy everything around them.

We did not tell Freddie until the day she arrived. Meg and I went to pick her up and bring her home. We walked down the path to where Freddie was with Julian and called out to him. He saw Daisy and said, "Who is that?" "This is your new dog who needs a home, she is yours." Freddie burst into tears and decided to call her Daisy.
XX

MARLEY

When I was growing up we always had a dog or two at home and one of them was an Irish Wolfhound named Jennie. She was huge, but the softest natured dog you could ever imagine. I was contacted about Marley as the family had a situation where one of their children became allergic to her hair. She needed a new home, so she came to the Ridge.

I honestly believe she is a little short sighted; she barks at you until she hears your voice or you come into focus, so I think she should probably be wearing glasses. That said, Marley spends most of her time asleep so probably does not really need them!

She is great friends with Daisy and they regularly get into trouble together, leading each other on. Normally on some massive hike which results in a telephone call from a local policeman letting Megan know that Daisy and Marley are currently hanging out in the local cemetery, someone's family lunch or anything else they can get into trouble with!
XX

DAISY

MARLEY

BARNEY BEAR AND HIS GIRLFRIEND EYEBROWS

This was another one of those situations where Julian was away filming and left with the strict instructions of "No more animals!" However, this had nothing to do with me.

After much discussion with Megan and Freddie, I agreed they could both walk home from school but if they were not back by 3pm I would be calling the police to look for them. I know, dramatic, but it's a big deal when they walk home on their own for the first time.

So by 3.15 pm, I was starting to have a breakdown when the front door goes and Freddie walks in, saying sorry they are late and not to be angry but something happened. My mind started running away with itself and then Megan appeared holding this tiny black and white puppy! My first reaction was "For heaven's sake, Megan, you know what Dad said. He is going to go mad!"

They then went on to tell me that a man was going to put him in the bin unless they took him home, so what could they do? I was furious, mainly because an adult has used children to offload his problem, so what else could we do? We had a new puppy. I sent a picture to Julian who instantly went nuts, but when he got home and held him in his hand (he was that small), he fell in love with him and Barney became a fixture of the Ridge.

He has grown into the worst behaved dog at the Ridge. His 'finest' hour was when he bought Eyebrows home. The chemistry between them both created a "pack effect" with all the dogs, which was just horrific.

Megan called her Eyebrows because, well, it is obvious really. She never quite got the idea of living with other animals. So, as I was now living in my own house, she came to live with me, where she now spends her days sleeping and eating.

XX

EYEBROWS

THIS IS SO QUICK AND EASY THAT YOU CAN WHIP THIS UP IN NO TIME AT ALL AFTER A BUSY DAY, SO DO GIVE IT A TRY!

PUTTANESCA

YOU WILL NEED

1 red onion, finely chopped (or a white onion if that is all you have)

4 cloves of garlic, finely chopped

½ a teaspoon of chili flakes

Handful of capers, chopped up small

Handful of black olives, chopped up small

Glass of red wine

Jar of sieved tomatoes (buy the best you can for this)

Salt

Black pepper

Zest of an orange

Handful of each fresh mint and parsley, finely chopped

Spaghetti

TO MAKE

1. First bring a big pan of water to the boil for your spaghetti and add lots of salt. When cooking pasta your water should be as salty as the Mediterranean and it should have room to move around; this avoids it all sticking together.

2. Whilst your spaghetti is cooking grab a large frying pan. Add a large glug of olive oil, your onions, salt and after about a minute, add your garlic.

3. Now add the chili flakes, capers, olives and mix around. Add your red wine and cook through for a few minutes. Then add your sieved tomatoes, more salt and freshly milled black pepper.

4. Drain your spaghetti. Just before you add it to the sauce, add the orange zest and chopped herbs. After, mix the spaghetti through.

5. Serve with a green salad and fresh bread to mop up any leftover sauce. Just delicious.

DIPS, SAUCES AND SPREADS!

CUCUMBER AND MINT SAUCE

YOU WILL NEED

Natural soy yogurt, I use four pots to make a big bowl, but adjust as you want

Handful of fresh mint finely chopped

½ a cucumber, or a whole Spanish cucumber, de-seeded and peeled. Then cut into small pieces

Salt and fresh black pepper

This can be used with curry, tagine, burgers or use it on jacket potatoes, in fact use it on anything, it is just delicious!

Super easy to make and takes just a few minutes to bring together.

TO MAKE

1. Mix all the ingredients in a bowl, add seasoning to taste, cover and put in the fridge. You can use it straight away but if you can leave it for about 30 minutes (at least), even better. It helps the mint absorb into the yogurt.

PESTO

YOU WILL NEED

Two handfuls of cashew nuts (no need to soak)

2 cloves of garlic

Big handful of fresh basil

½ a cup of nutritional yeast

½ a cup of ground almonds

Salt

Pepper

Extra Virgin Olive Oil

Super easy to make and no need at all to use expensive pine nuts (which cost a fortune!). I use cashews to make mine.

TO MAKE

1. Put all the ingredients in the food processor except the oil.

2. Blend and then add the oil until you reach the consistency you want. You want it like a paste, not runny.

Note: Instead of basil, you can also use fresh coriander for a different taste. Rocket also works really well for another taste.

VEGAN PARMESAN CHEESE

YOU WILL NEED

Nutritional yeast

Ground almonds

Salt, to taste

Three ingredients and incredibly easy. It will also sit in a jar for ages!

TO MAKE

1. Mix equal amounts of nutritional yeast and ground almonds. Add salt to taste. You can then use this as you need it.

2. If you want to do something really special, mix some of the mix with a little bit of water to create a paste. Then, spread thinly, onto baking paper and pop into a low oven until crisp, this creates delicious parmesan crisps!

Sweetpea and Megan

SWEETPEA!

Where to begin with Sweetpea! I guess first, you need to imagine in your head the soundtrack of *Jaws*... I know that for many, even when she was tiny, this is what they heard as they walked around the Ridge!

Sweetpea's Mum is Mia; who had, lets just say, an *encounter* with a wild pig. The result; half wild boar piglets! One night they disappeared, all except one. Upon closer inspection it became clear that Mia was not producing any milk so, the only way to save the remaining piglet was to remove her and hand rear her. Now that may sound easy, but Mia is big and was super protective of her piglet, so this was going to be a challenge.

The only thing in my favour is that the pigs trust me, so I was going to have to use this and try to remove the piglet without too much stress to either Mia or the little one. Meg and I went to work to rescue the piglet.

It took some doing and some very fast running at one point, but we managed to remove the piglet to give her a fighting chance of survival. Megan became her surrogate Mum, something she has done many times before and something she has a natural ability for, mainly due to her love of pigs and animals.

So now Megan had the task of feeding this little piglet every hour and making sure she was warm and felt safe, which translates into she sleeps in your bed with you under your chin. Wherever you are, so is the piglet.

Megan trained her to drink from a bottle and very soon she would chase Megan around, demanding her feed. Meg went through so many long, long nights with her, but this stripy little piglet was getting stronger and with that strength came her personality.

Even when she could be held in one hand she was a terror. She would chase people around, nipping at their feet, and it would not be uncommon to see someone running, with a tiny piglet chasing them, or someone standing on a chair yelling for help. The new phase around the Ridge became "Where is Sweetpea?"

Megan and Sweetpea have the biggest bond. She has grown and continues to grow into a beautiful pig. She likes some people. Luckily I am one of them, but everyone else, beware!

She now has her own beautiful run where she can be safe. Actually, it is more about keeping everyone else safe. When there are no volunteers she can run around the land, chasing the dogs, chasing horses, chasing other pigs and of course, chasing people. In fact, she just goes wild which, considering her father, is not surprising.

At the end of the day, we all love Sweetpea and Sweetpea... well, she loves Megan.

XX

DIPS, SAUCES AND SPREADS!

MAYONNAISE

YOU WILL NEED

Soy milk, I use half a pack

Extra virgin olive oil

Apple cider vinegar, just a splash

Juice of half a lemon

1 teaspoon of dijon mustard

Salt

Every vegan mayo I have seen has been incredibly expensive and to be honest, not particularly tasty. With a food processor you can make delicious mayo at a fraction of the cost.

TO MAKE

1. Put everything, except the oil, into a blender and blend once to mix all the ingredients. Then, whilst still blending on low, slowly add the oil until you reach the consistency of mayo. Check the taste and add more salt if needed and that is it! It keeps in the fridge, in an airtight container for a month.

GARLIC MAYONNAISE / AIOLI

YOU WILL NEED

3-4 cloves of garlic

Mayonnaise (see above)

This is so delicious that you find yourself putting it on everything! I like to add chives to this too, but only add it to the mayo you are going to use as it will not keep in the fridge, in fact, you can add all sorts to the mayo, just experiment!

TO MAKE

1. To make garlic mayo just pop three, or four, cloves of garlic into the blender first, blend to chop up and then carry on with the standard mayonnaise recipe. Try it on everything!

CHILI & MANGO SALSA

YOU WILL NEED

1 ripe mango

6 or 7 fresh mint leaves

1 red chili de-seeded and finely chopped or chili flakes

Zest and juice of one lime

Salt & Black Pepper

This is so easy and yet it is something that everyone loves and wants the recipe for, so here it is!

TO MAKE

1. Peel and chop your mango and put into a bowl.

2. Chop your mint leaves and add to bowl.

3. Add your chili, zest and juice to the bowl. Then add salt and pepper.

4. Mix together and it's ready! See, I said it was easy.

DIPS, SAUCES AND SPREADS!

PEANUT BUTTER

YOU WILL NEED

Peanuts – I always get two bags of salted nuts as I prefer the taste but you can use whichever you prefer.

This is another ingredient that seems to be incredibly expensive and so many contain palm oil which is something I avoid, so here is a super easy recipe to make your own. You will need a processor for this one.

TO MAKE

1. Put in a processor and blend. First it goes into bits, then smaller bits, then it looks like it is never going to change. The oils will then start to be released from the nuts and you start to see peanut butter! I have to do this in stages to avoid blowing up my processor (learnt from experience)

2. Once it is smooth, just pop in a jar and it is ready to use. Much easier and no nasty hidden ingredients.

VEGAN CHOCOLATE SPREAD

YOU WILL NEED

2 handfuls of hazelnuts

1 Tablespoon of cocoa powder

A splash of vanilla extract

TO MAKE

You use the same method as above but this time use hazelnuts! Add a splash of vanilla extract (only use extract not essence) and a Tablespoon of cocoa powder or more if you want. Blend in the same way and you have chocolate spread!

RONNIE

RONNIE AND STEVE

I have a soft spot for donkeys. I think it is the connection between that acceptance of bad behaviour, of people just expecting them to get on with it – to bounce back, which donkeys do. They take the abuse, the cruelty and continue on, but if you look into their eyes you can see the sadness.

RONNIE

I first met Ronnie when I was with Julian, working out a way to rescue the herd of horses that a... let's say "farmer", had grown tired of. I started to look around the property. There was a huge shed to the back of the land, which looked like storage; but upon entering I found, standing in an area not much bigger than him, Ronnie.

Shut in the dark, standing in a ton of crap, he looked incredibly sad. I stroked him and talked to him. He was adorable. I went straight outside and asked about him.

He was described as aggressive and not a nice donkey at all, hence he was separated from everyone else. I asked if I could buy him. "No", was the reply. I went straight back in and whispered in Ronnie's ear, "I have no idea how long this is going to take, but I am going to get you out of here."

The weeks passed and I kept asking if we could buy him. The reply was always no until one day there was a pause before the word no. I knew that money would work, but money was short. Money equals food for the animals and I knew it had to be something significant to make this happen.

Julian set to work and thanks to our supporters we raised enough money in about one hour to offer to the farmer. We went back and asked again, this time, holding a roll of money. He agreed!

Ronnie, we thought would be an excellent companion for Nero, however, it became clear very quickly that Nero was having none of it. He hated him from the start and actually never got over that, but the important thing was Ronnie was out of that shed and in the fresh air.

It turned out that Ronnie was taken out of the shed at weekends where the family would get him drunk until he fell over which was a great source of entertainment for them. It was no wonder he was grumpy and aggressive. He is none of those things. He loves people, he is kind and best of all he is free of abuse.

STEVE

Some people never learn, no matter how much you try to educate them and to help them see the error of their ways. When I saw Steve standing in exactly the same place as Ronnie had been, I knew we had to do something.

This poor young donkey clearly had no love. Stuck, just like Ronnie, in a dark shed, knee deep in filth, an empty bucket where water should be and just a crack in the door when the tiniest glimmer of light shone through. He was just another "toy" for weekend entertainment.

Again, I whispered to him that he would come and live with us, that we would find a way. It was the same situation, no, the owner would not let us have him, they wanted him. We kept on asking and asking, but he was adamant; no.

Steve arrived in the most magical way. We had loads of volunteers with us and suddenly I heard donkeys calling. Now, just like children, you recognise your own children's cries and donkeys are the same. In the middle of all this noise was a donkey I did not recognise.

We looked down into the field and there, standing in the middle was Steve! He had escaped from the farm and found his way, across several fields, to us and was letting us all know he was here. It is how he got his name – Steve McQueen from the Great Escape!

We walked over to him and found him a place to go. Everyone was excited but also upset that he may have to go back to the farm he came from. I remember poor Indie being heartbroken at that prospect, but it was never going to happen.

Julian and I went over to the farm and basically told him, "Your donkey has escaped, he is with us and he is staying there", to which he replied – and I will never forget this – "I don't care, I have others".

STEVE

For several days, Steve just looked out across the land, as if completely mesmerised by being outdoors with fresh air, fresh water and lots of food.

He found his way to us because he knew where he wanted to live, at the Ridge. It later came out that he would regularly have marijuana smoke blown up his nose because it was "funny". Some people are simply disgusting.

Nero hated Steve. They would call to each other across the fields. I am sure; no, positive that they were swearing and insulting each other all day. Basically they were just rude to one another!

So remember, when you make a promise to a donkey, never let them down.

SIDES AND EXTRA TIPS

Here we have some of the dishes I use to complement other dishes. For me, the idea of having a selection of foods to add to your meal makes all the difference.

I have included a basic sauce, it really is the best start for so many different recipes. It is great just as it is, but once you get into the hang of doing this you can pretty much knock up anything very quickly and of course, make extra and split it – that way you can make a bolognese, a chili and a curry without too much fuss.

BASIC SAUCE

YOU WILL NEED

1 onion

1 celery stalk

1 leek

Garlic

Any other veg (optional)

1 jar lentils, chickpeas or beans

2 jars sieved tomatoes

Spices

TO MAKE

1. Chop up an onion, celery, leek, garlic and anything else you have to hand such as an aubergine or courgette and gently fry in a little oil until soft. Now add a jar of lentils, chickpeas or any beans, mix it up even. Toss them around in the vegetables. Add salt, pepper, oregano, paprika and a vegetable stock cube.

2. Now add two jars of sieved tomatoes, enough to cover the mixture and stir through. Let it just simmer for a few minutes and then it is ready. If it seems too thick add a little water.

3. Change the flavours by adding curry powder when you fry the vegetables, or chilli flakes, to create a curry base or a chilli con veg base.

4. Once you have this base you can always add other things, for example, leftover cooked potatoes can be added to create more of a casserole. Serve with rice or couscous and lots of salad or vegetables.

DELICIOUS POTATOES

YOU WILL NEED

Potatoes

Olive oil

Sea salt

Rosemary, fresh or dried

Garlic

2 lemons

TO MAKE

1. Chop potatoes in half, do more than you need because these work cold and can be added to other things too.

2. Put in a baking tray with lots of olive oil, sea salt, fresh or dried rosemary, cloves of garlic still in their skins and two lemons cut in half. Put your hands in and give it all a good mix, put in the oven, high, until the potatoes are crispy and cooked through. You can now squeeze the garlic out of its skin and mix into the olive oil. You can use some of this when you eat the potatoes, but with the fantastic taste it will have, save it to mix into couscous or cooked rice, which is why you need to be a little generous with the oil! You can also add chili flakes to this at the beginning if you want a different taste too.

SIDES AND EXTRA TIPS

SIMPLE NAAN BREAD

YOU WILL NEED

Flour

Salt

Olive oil

TO MAKE

1. In a food processor, add flour until it is about half full. Then add salt, a glug of olive oil and you can add additional spices too if you wish. Then pour cold water slowly into the mixture with the processor on, until it forms a soft ball of dough.

2. Break the dough into pieces, roll out flat, as thin as you can. With a splash of olive oil heated in a frying pan, lay the dough into the pan until you see the bubbles forming and then turn over.

3. These make a fab replacement for bread and can be used as wraps, You can also use them for dips.

BUTTER BEAN PÂTÉ

YOU WILL NEED

1-2 jars butter beans

4 cloves garlic

1 teaspoon paprika

½ teaspoon dried chili flakes

1 teaspoon oregano

Juice of 2 limes

A few mint leaves

Salt and freshly milled black pepper

This is just delicious on a million things but for me. I love it on jacket potatoes; it just brings something awesome to the dish, as well as protein, so do give this a go. It is incredibly easy and everyone, so far, loves it!

TO MAKE

1. Just put one jar, or two if you want to make extra, of butter beans without the liquid into a food processor, along with four cloves of garlic, a teaspoon of paprika, half a teaspoon of dried chili flakes, teaspoon of oregano, juice of two limes and a few mint leaves. Add salt and freshly milled black pepper. Whizz together slowly adding olive oil until you have a pate consistency. Test for seasoning and that's it, done. Try a spoonful of this in the bottom of stuffed peppers, tomatoes or as an alternative topping on your pizza.

SPICY FXXXXXG SPINACH!!! - FOR SHAUNA

YOU WILL NEED

1 bag baby spinach

2 cloves garlic

1 dessert spoon of curry powder

Olive oil

2 jars of sieved tomatoes

Salt and pepper

Sunflower seeds, to garnish

This dish got its name after being asked at least one million times what it was, because everyone loved it and wanted it. Despite actually having written on the wall what it was, people still kept asking. The last to ask was Shauna and through this she created its new name!

TO MAKE

1. In a large frying pan add a glug of oil and a large dessert spoon of curry powder. Just heat through and then add chopped garlic, around two cloves, salt and pepper and mix through.

2. Now add two jars of sieved tomatoes and once hot, add a bag of baby spinach leaves. Take off the heat and mix through and then sprinkle with sunflower seeds. Done.

SIDES AND EXTRA TIPS

AVO SPLASH

YOU WILL NEED per person

1 avocado

½ a lemon

Olive oil

Chili flakes

Salt and pepper

This makes a super alternative to just having sliced avocado on your salad or if you want to create something a little special in your presentation.

TO MAKE

1. In a food processor add your avocado, one per person and blitz. Now add salt, pepper and the juice of around half a lemon for each avo but taste as you go, a pinch of chili flakes and blitz again. Now add olive oil as you blitz until you have a pouring, but thick, consistency. This is now ready to go. You can drizzle over salad or put a blob on a plate and drag a spoon down to give a "splash" on your plate. Delicious!

GUACAMOLE

YOU WILL NEED

1 avocado

Lemon juice

Chili flakes

Salt and pepper

This is something else that I have no idea why people buy. It is just so easy to make and can be whizzed up in seconds, in fact, you can do this with a fork if your avos are ripe, so no more excuses, make your own!

TO MAKE

1. Mash your avocados with a fork or in the processor and add salt, black pepper, lemon juice and a couple of pinches of dried chili flakes. Done. Absolutely no need to buy this ready made!

KALE CHIPS

YOU WILL NEED

Kale

Salt

Oil (optional)

Spices (optional)

Kale has not yet reached Spain yet but it grows very easily and you can buy it in most places so do try this. I like to make them and then crumble them over salad for an extra nutritional boost. If you make them in a dehydrator, at 105 degrees, they maintain all their nutritional value, but you can do them in an oven, just have it on super, super low so they dry out.

TO MAKE

1. Prepare your kale leaves by washing and then putting on a baking tray or dehydrator tray. Then sprinkle with salt and pop in to dry out. I like to rub them first with a little coconut oil and then add the salt but this also means you can add different flavours through spice or lemon juice. They are just so delicious and once dry you can keep them in a jar to use later.

2. You can also deep fry them for an instant garnish. I do this for putting into burgers, so this is a great "speedy" option. Be careful and make sure your leaves are dry before adding to the oil or you will have hot oil spitting everywhere! Once they come out of the fryer add the seasoning to them whilst still hot and carefully toss around. Then, put onto kitchen roll to absorb any leftover oil.

BILL AND BEN

BILL AND BEN

I cannot tell you how many messages we get each week with requests for us to take animals; from an individual pig to groups of over 50 pigs, horses, donkeys, goats and dogs. In fact, the list is endless and it is always heartbreaking when we have to say no, but in the case of Bill and Ben we knew we had to find a way.

We had reached the situation where we had to look at each case and see what the real reason was behind asking us to take animals. In so many cases, it was about owners becoming bored, or not having done their research on a particular animal before taking them on. So, in those cases, we tried to help them find different solutions to re-home or to better understand the needs of the animals. With Bill & Ben, no one was interested in their long term well being, except a group of exceptional Spanish people who found and rescued them, without thinking about what to do next and contacted us.

Bill and Ben were found in a shed. When the doors opened, it was full of it was full of dead, abandoned piglets. No one knows what happened exactly, but in the middle of all these dead pigs were two survivors... Bill & Ben.

They were rescued and taken away from the hell hole they had been left in. They were 8 weeks old.

They then had to go on a journey to get to us. Everyone pulled together and made it happen. I remember the day they arrived. It was incredible. They came running up the drive greeting everyone, just like a dog would; they were so happy. This incredible group of rescuers had done a fantastic job of showing them love and kindness. They had no fear of humans, none at all.

It was an amazing day.

Their new run was set up behind Steve and Prospero. It was small enough that we could keep an eye on them, but big enough to allow them movement. Ben had sustained an injury whilst he was in the shed, a dislocated hip. It was important that he had movement but not too much so that as he gained weight, it would not cause any issues to the injury.

Steve instantly fell in love with Bill & Ben and they would often be seen chatting over the fence together!

They grew stronger each day. In fact, you could see them gaining weight daily. They both have very different personalities. Bill is very sensible and Ben, well let's just say, he is not quite as bright as Bill!

Sadly, their tails had been cut and their teeth clipped, but apart from that, they were in great health.

They loved to sleep on you, but I had to insist that we did not encourage this too much. Great while they are little, but these boys are going to end up being around 600 pounds and you do not want that just "flopping" onto you!

I had to remind myself when they were six months old that at this point they would have gone into the food chain. These two boys, full of life, fun and excitement, would have had a very different life had it not been for those wonderful people finding them both. Looking into their very human eyes, you can only imagine the horror that pigs suffer whilst being transported and then, finally, to be murdered for meat. I would say to anyone that feels they "cannot live without bacon" to really spend time with pigs and understand their intelligence, their individual personalities and their similarities to humans and then, ask yourself if you still feel the same.

Now at over a year old they are living a life they would never have had. They would be gone by now... eaten.

Bill & Ben are both real characters. They are strong, playful, they cause chaos on a daily basis, they love good food, they like to visit the other animals. In fact, they love life, but the best bit: they are two very happy pigs who now, just by being, show others why pigs are friends, not food.

XX

SLOW COOKED RED CABBAGE

YOU WILL NEED

1 whole red cabbage
Remove stalk and shred the leaves.
I use a food processor for this but a
sharp knife is just as effective.

Zest and juice from 2 large oranges

Zest and juice from 1 large lemon

1 large red onion, finely chopped

2 cloves of garlic, finely chopped

Handful of sultanas

2 glasses of red wine

2 teaspoons of dried rosemary or a
couple of stalks of fresh rosemary

Dessert spoon of cinnamon

½ a jar of organic cranberry sauce

Salt & pepper

¼ teaspoon of chili flakes, or a small
pinch

1 jar of apple puree, or you can add
two dessert apples finely chopped;
they will breakdown

Glug of oil

Water

I love this either raw or cooked, but if you are going to cook it then take your time. It is a beautiful vegetable but it needs love to create the perfect red cabbage. I normally serve this with nut roast or my veggie wellie and make this anytime, not just at Christmas! The joy is you can leave it to simmer away and get on with the rest of your life whilst your home is filled with simply delicious aromas. I use a whole cabbage because I like to freeze down half of it, saves time, so whilst this sounds like I am cooking for 25, there is method in my madness!

TO MAKE

1. In a large pan, add a glug of oil and then add the onion, garlic, spices and herbs. Warm through. When hot add the cabbage and mix through.

2. Now add the wine and mix again. Add the zest and juice of the oranges and lemon, the apple and cranberry sauce, sultanas and then add lots of salt and pepper. Now add a small amount of water, just to loosen it all up a little, but do not cover it all in water, so start with a glass and go from there.

3. Bring to the boil and then reduce to the lowest it will go, put a lid on it and walk away. Every now and then have a quick check, stir and put the lid back on. I normally let this do its thing for at least an hour, but two is better. Taste it and check the seasoning, once you are happy, take the lid off and let it just reduce a little and then it is ready!

WINNIE WOO

Let me first start by saying: just as Elvis is the King, Winnie is the Queen – no question, she rules and she rules everyone.

In the world of pigs, there is a very strict system. Everyone has their place. This understanding starts at birth, as soon as a piglet is born it finds its way to their teat. Now, the closer to their Mum's head the teat is the better the milk, so the first born gets the first choice and so it goes down the line. This is their first lesson in knowing your place.

Now, at the top of each herd is the head male and the head female, but it is the female who ultimately rules everyone, and Winnie Woo... well, she takes her job very seriously!

Winnie Woo was once the companion of Hamilton, but she has since moved on and now rules over Elvis, poor thing, and keeps him in check. Every now and then he rebels, but he soon puts him back in his place and he carries on his way, grumbling all the way.

Having said that, Winnie Woo has left a lasting impression with many people, I have even been sent photographs of tattoos of Winnie Woo because people found her such an inspiration so whatever she is doing, she is doing it well!

One thing you should know about pigs, they never forget anything. If someone is horrible to them they may not react at that very moment, but they remember and when the time is right, then they retaliate. So when you hear people saying a pig attacked and it was completely unprovoked, that is not true – they were just biding their time for payback. So, with Winnie Woo, she remembers where she began and has never quite got over it.

Winnie Woo was purchased as a piglet and taken back to a house where she had full run and used the shower as a toilet. I know; gross! So to Winnie Woo, she should be living in a house with a full fridge and total access to the sofa whenever required. However, pigs need to be outside, not only to be with other pigs, but there are certain minerals they can only find in soil, so no matter how well she was looked after, to maintain perfect health she needed to be outside. So, she went to live with Hammy and his family and ultimately, she came to live with us.

She can be a very strong character but you need to understand with pigs that you must always be in control, so when she pushes you, you push back. You have to let her know that she cannot control you and then all is well. It is an understanding you have between you. I appreciate that she is in charge of all the pigs but she also understands that she cannot boss me around, either.

Winnie Woo and Elvis spend all their time together, sitting under the fig tree mainly, where they watch and keep an eye on what is going on. They appear to be asleep but if you arrive with treats you will see how quickly they are up on their feet and heading over; Elvis in his usual relaxed state and Winnie Woo knocking everyone out the way until she gets to you. She then gives you a look of being the sweetest pig that ever lived and therefore you should give everything directly to her.

If you have seen the video on the Pig Village Facebook page, you will see how gentle she is as she steals pears out of my pocket and I never knew until I watched the video!

She is just a lady who knows what she wants and how to get it so I am not surprised she inspires people. I know she inspires me.

xx

THIS IS SO EASY AND DELICIOUS. YOU CAN CHANGE THE ACTUAL TASTE OF THE CHEESECAKE SO EASILY.

VEGAN CHEESECAKE

YOU WILL NEED

For the base

Half a cup of dates

Half a cup of prunes

One cup of nuts
I use a mix of walnuts and pecans, but you can use all walnuts or hazelnuts. The only one which does not seem to work very well is peanuts but if you have a few packs of nuts around then just use up what you have.

For the topping

200 g pre-soaked cashews, normally this is about one packet

Juice of one large lemon

80 ml of melted coconut oil

159 ml of coconut milk

120 ml of maple syrup, you can use agave if you prefer

1 teaspoon of vanilla extract

One tub of fresh blueberries or the flavour of your choice

In the picture I have created a blueberry cheesecake topped with salted cashew brittle, but you can change the blueberries for fresh strawberries, raspberries, lemon zest, peanut butter, vegan chocolate spread or you can go crazy and try it with fresh herbs! Mint and lemon is delicious. Just experiment and the great joy is you can freeze this so I make it in a tray, slice it into pieces and freeze so, you can take a piece out, make a coffee and by the time you sit down it is ready to eat, plus, it is completely raw so actually quite healthy!

I never remember to soak cashews the night before for anything, but you can put the cashews in a bowl and cover in boiling water and in two hours they are ready to use, so much easier and better for those of us who forget everything!

TO MAKE

1. Start with the base. In your food processor, blitz your nuts until they are crumbs and then remove and put to one side. Now add your dates, prunes and blitz until chopped. Tip the nuts back in and blitz again so it all combines.

2. Now push this mix down into a loose leaf cake tin.

For the topping

3. Put all the ingredients in your food processor and blitz until smooth. If it seems to be too thick then you can add more maple syrup or more lemon juice until it is all silky and smooth. Then add your pot of blueberries just leaving a few for decoration. Now pour over your base and pop into the fridge to set or into the freezer if you are in a rush! Once it has set a little, I then take a sharp knife and divide it into pieces so it is easy to serve!

I have topped with salted cashew brittle which is super easy. Just heat a frying pan and add a handful of cashews. Carefully toast them and then cover with sugar, a teaspoon of salt and leave it until you see the sugar starting to melt. Move the sugar around with a wooden spoon, but be super careful; this stuff really burns if you get it on yourself! Once it has all melted pour onto a lightly greased board. I actually do it directly onto the kitchen worktop. Once it has cooled, you can slide a knife underneath it and then break it up into pieces. It will keep in an airtight container for ages, but honestly, it will not last five minutes!

I LOVE MAKING THIS, IF ONLY BECAUSE IT IS REALLY JUST A HUGE BOWL OF FRUIT THAT FEELS LIKE ICE CREAM AND YET, IS JUST ALL NATURAL, SO YOU CAN STUFF YOURSELF SILLY ON THIS AND ACTUALLY BE DOING YOURSELF SOME GOOD AT THE SAME TIME!

VEGAN ICE CREAM

YOU WILL NEED

4 ripe bananas, peeled, sliced and frozen solid

For the flavours pictured

Vanilla extract

Fresh berries

Vegan mint chocolate

 **TIP**

Other Ideas

Soak some sultanas in rum, then chop up and add to the basic mix along with some crushed up vegan biscuits for a delicious after dinner ice cream. Use fruits in season such as peaches, mango and a personal favourite of mine toasted pistachio.

Just think of your favourite ice cream, use the bananas as a base and create away!

So, the basic start to vegan ice cream, for me anyway, is bananas. Just peeled, sliced and into the freezer until solid. Now some people blitz just this, but for me, it lacks something, it is not creamy enough, more like, well, baby food, so I add a few other bits and bobs to create a real whippy style ice cream.

Every option here starts with the frozen banana. You can use four bananas which will give you enough for two people, but experiment. To be honest, this would probably do for four but we really like it! Make sure you bananas are ripe, if they are under-ripe you will never achieve the right consistency, they need to be soft before they are put into freeze.

You will need a food processor or a really good hand blender for this.

TO MAKE

Take your bananas out of the freezer, if they are super hard, just leave them for about 10 to 15 minutes before blending. Then put into your food processor or a big bowl and blend until smooth. Now this is your base from which to create all types of ice cream.

Vanilla

Just the basic banana mix with a few drops of vanilla extract added. Delicious with just about everything!

Raspberry

Just blend up fresh raspberries and add them to the banana mix. When these are in season I buy and freeze them so you can make this at anytime.

Blueberry

Blend fresh blueberries and add to the banana mix. As before, buy in season and freeze.

Chocolate Mint

Super easy, buy vegan mint chocolate, melt and mix through the banana mix.

THIS IS MY GO TO EVERY TIME. IT LITERALLY TAKES 10 MINUTES TO PREPARE AND WITH A LITTLE IMAGINATION YOU CAN CREATE SO MANY DIFFERENT TASTES.

LEMON DRIZZLE CAKE

YOU WILL NEED

Self raising flour 275g / 10 oz

Caster Sugar 200g / 7 oz

Baking Powder 2 teaspoons

Zest and juice of one large lemon

100ml of vegetable oil

170 ml of cold water

Teaspoon of vanilla extract (not essence!)

For the icing

150g / 5 oz icing sugar

Lemon juice

This is a simple recipe that can be adapted to create many different flavours. It starts as a lemon drizzle cake but can then be created into a whole variety of tastes, but always use this recipe and add to it, you need the lemon juice in the mix to make it all work!

You can make one whole cake or you can split it into individual portions, use a mould and then you can fill them with all sorts of delicious fruits. Start with the basic recipe and go from there! Experiment, it is how we find new tastes.

Now, sadly, you do need to measure your ingredients for making cakes, but as time goes on you just get a feel and you will no longer need to weigh out ingredients, thankfully. I really hate anything that involves having to mess about with weights and measures!

TO MAKE

1. Heat your oven to 200 and then either line a cake tin, put cases in a bun tin or, using a vegan spray, spray your mini cake moulds.

2. Simply put your flour, baking powder, sugar, vanilla extract and lemon zest in a bowl and then add your oil, juice and water. Mix everything together and that's it, all done!.

3. Now tip into your choice of tins or cases and put in the oven, it will take around 25 minutes for the full size version and about 15 to 20 minutes for the individual versions, just keep checking them after 15 minutes.

4. Once cooked, let the cakes cool and then you are ready to add your icing glaze. Just mix the icing sugar with a little lemon juice until it is the right consistency to pour and drizzle over. Done!

VARIATIONS

Chocolate Jaffa Cake

Replace two tablespoons of the flour with cocoa powder and the zest of two oranges. Prepare in the same way but for the topping use orange juice to make the glaze. I like to top this with a little more orange zest too.

Blueberry Buns

Using a mould, make the lemon drizzle cake in the same way but add a handful of fresh blueberries into the mix. Do not go mad with this or the blueberries will produce too much juice and your cakes will just be mush. Save extra for serving with the buns or if you have suitable moulds you can chop them and fill the middles with fresh blueberries. You can do the same with raspberries, which work wonderfully well with the lemony taste.

Walnut

Add a handful of walnuts to the mix and cook in the same way and whilst it is in the oven toast a few more and then chop up to scatter over your glaze.

So many different options that you can create from this recipe so give it a go!

Lemon Drizzle Cake

Blueberry buns

LITTLE RED

PROSPERO

LITTLE RED AND PROSPERO

Little Red and Prospero came to live with us from a very happy life, but sadly a situation in the family he lived with meant they had to be rehomed. So, another connection from Hamilton; they came to live with us.

Now these two little falabella horses arrived full of spirit. They may only be 30cms tall, but in their mind they are strapping stallions and acted accordingly.

They arrived and joined Jacob and Nero, who both found them quite, well... lets say, 'interesting'. For a while, they all lived happily together.

It soon became clear that both of them had a power over Jacob and he was getting bullied. Yes, I know, but this is Jacob, so they were moved to their own paddock.

They were best friends and then, one day, they decided they hated each other. So again, it was time to separate and move them both.

Little Red was put with Nero where they actually became great friends. Little Red could boss Nero around and he did not seem to mind. Prospero went with Steve – same situation. It all seemed to work very well.

Both Little Red and Prospero were absolute terrors. They would break out of their runs and head for the herd. Little Red was the worst. He would get into the herd, split them up and then guard over the water so no one could drink. He would chase Jacob around and basically cause all kinds of issues until one day during one of his escapades, he got kicked and his leg was broken.

The vet arrived and it was clear that this was going to be a long journey, but everything was done to try and save Little Red.

He went into surgery for 7 hours where they fitted a metal plate and then it was a waiting game to see if this would work for him.

He showed great signs of healing and then disaster struck. Infection attacked and had worked its way into his bones. The tragic decision was made to release him from any more pain and stress and he was put to sleep.

Little Red now rests next to his best friend Nero and we like to think of them both running around together, causing as much chaos as they did here on earth.

NOTES

THESE PAGES ARE FOR YOU TO REALLY MAKE THIS BOOK YOUR OWN. CREATE VARIATIONS ON THE RECIPES, ADD PHOTOS, SHARE THEM AND ENJOY THEM. TELL YOUR OWN STORIES ABOUT FAMILY, COOKING OR ANIMALS. ALWAYS REMEMBER, COOKING IS LOVE MADE VISIBLE.

NOTES

NOTES

NOTES

NOTES

NOTES

FOR **NERO**
A LASTING TRIBUTE

As well as dedicating this book to Nero, I wanted to do something else in his name that would help other donkeys, mules and horses around the world. Nero was a rescue and I know he would want to help others in awful situations too.

I have researched the options and I've finally settled with **www.thebrooke.org**. Brooke is an international animal welfare charity dedicated to improving the lives of working horses, donkeys and mules. Operating in Africa, Asia, Latin America and the Middle East, they reach over 1.8 million working horses, donkeys and mules – more than any other organisation.

How they came to be is a fascinating story. On arrival in Egypt in 1930, Dorothy Brooke was determined to find the surviving ex-warhorses of the British, Australian and American forces. These brave and noble horses were sold into a life of hard labour in Cairo when conflict ended.

Searching for them throughout Cairo, Dorothy was appalled to find hundreds of emaciated and worn-out animals desperately in need of help. She wrote a letter to the Morning Post (which later became the Daily Telegraph) exposing their plight. The public were so moved they sent her the equivalent of £20,000 in today's money to help end the suffering of these once proud horses.

Within three years, Dorothy Brooke had purchased five thousand ex-warhorses. Most were old, exhausted and had to be humanely put down, but thanks to her compassion they ended their lives peacefully. Dorothy Brooke knew thousands of hard working horses, donkeys and mules were still suffering, so in 1934 she founded the Old War Horse Memorial Hospital in Cairo, with the promise of free veterinary care for all the city's working horses and donkeys.

The Brooke Hospital for Animals was born. You can read more of the story on their website, and it is the perfect example how one person can make change. I know Dorothy Brooke would have loved Nero too, so please support their work in Nero's name through his tribute page, **nero.muchloved.com**.

BROOKE
ACTION FOR WORKING
HORSES AND DONKEYS

Share your stories, photos and memories of Nero

and if you wish, make a donation to help other donkeys, mules and horses in need around the world by visiting

nero.muchloved.com

INDEX

SPECIAL THANK YOU

For the last 23 years I have shared my life with someone very special. Together we went on numerous adventures, did crazy things, built a family, moved to Spain, followed our dreams and ultimately, we ended up creating Jacobs Ridge.

Those 23 years were full of love, laughter, madness and proving to the world that you can achieve anything. If I wrote a book on our life together, no one would believe it!

Now I begin a new chapter of my life, but I will never forget those years. And I know, God willing, when I find myself sitting back in the years to come, I will look back on all these years and laugh again, cry again but above all, cherish all the moments, the memories and the love.

Know that when you walk alone and you feel a breeze cross your face, that is my spirit that will stay with you wherever you are. Thank you for everything. Be happy, be strong, be you.
For now, I am putting all those memories into a box and tying it up with ribbon.

XX